The Twenty-first Century Church:

Is It Waxing or Waning?

James Perry

The Twenty-first Century Church: Is It Waxing or Waning

Copyright © 2015 by James Perry

Published by:
Theocentric Publishing Group
1069A Main Street
Chipley, FL 32428

www.theocentricpublishing.com

All rights reserved. No part of this book may be reproduced or transmitted in any form or by any means without written permission of the author.

Unless otherwise noted, the Scriptural Quotations are taken from the New American Standard Bible. Scripture taken from the NEW AMERICAN STANDARD BIBLE®,Copyright © 1960, 1962, 1963, 1968, 1971, 1972, 1973, 1975, 1977, 1995 by The Lockman Foundation. Used by permission
Other Versions Used
The New King James Version (NKJV), © 1982 by Thomas Nelson, Inc. All rights reserved. Used within Guideline Permission.
The Holy Bible, English Standard Version® (ESV®) Copyright © 2001 by Crossway. Used within Guideline Permission.
New International Version, THE HOLY BIBLE, NEW INTERNATIONAL VERSION®, NIV® Copyright © 1973, 1978, 1984, 2011 by Biblica, Inc.™ All rights reserved worldwide. Used within Guideline Permission.
New Living Translation (NLT), Scripture quotations are taken from the *Holy Bible*, New Living Translation, copyright ©1996, 2004, 2007, 2013 by Tyndale House Foundation. Used within Guideline Permission of Tyndale House Publishers, Inc., Carol Stream, Illinois 60188.

Library of Congress Control Number: 2015942682

ISBN 9780986405525

DEDICATION

A question that is sometimes considered, especially in religious efforts (missionary and para-church groups) or church ministry, is: How many great servants of God do you personally know? An additional question that might be coupled with this is: What does it take to make you want to quit? The idea of the questions is a focus upon the task one is called to do. It can be a very lonely, misunderstood or under-appreciated work. It may even be a task where the merits of it may be questioned and the costs of it discouraged. When I think of the men and women over the years who have committed themselves to serve the Lord anywhere, at any time and at any cost, my mind focuses on the faculty of the schools I was privileged to attend.

Columbia Bible College (now Columbia International University) in Columbia, SC was the place of my initial preparation for ministry in the years 1954-57. The school had a faculty of godly men and women who sacrificially gave of their time and effort to prepare the students for the varying kind of ministry opportunities as missionaries, translators or pastors. It was the place where the Lord brought my wife and I together with a united desire to serve the Lord the rest of our lives. The words of a hymn written by Margaret Clarkson (1938) became part of the inspiration and challenge of serving the Lord and to live a life of triumphal praise to Him. She wrote these meaningful and purposeful words that include: "So send I you to labor unrewarded…to toil for me alone…As the Father hath sent Me, so send I you!"

In 1958, my young family and I moved to St. Louis, MO where a new Presbyterian College and Seminary had begun. Once again, it meant being in the presence of gifted and dedicated men and women, some of whom had come out of retirement, to train another generation of servants for the Lord. In the years of 1958-64, foundational principles and values were instilled that have lasted a lifetime. Many times, dedicated men and women can be overlooked or taken for granted. In an entry (March 12, 2015) at: *www.thisday.pcahistory.org*, there was a perceptive statement shared: "If we were to list the number of ministers who have come and gone without any great notice by the visible church except to note their birth dates, years and place of training, some bare record of what churches or schools they were at, and the date of their death, the list would be unending. The great majority of God's servants fall into this category. Perhaps you, reader, fall into this listing. Unnoticed by the world, not mentioned by denominational magazines, your name would be one such pastor or teacher. But, there is another record being written which is of greater importance. Found in Malachi 3:16-17, the prophet writes: "Then those who feared the Lord-spoke with one another. The Lord paid attention and heard them, and a book of remembrance was written before him who feared the Lord and esteemed his name. They shall be mine, says the Lord of hosts, in the day when I make up my treasured possession, and I will spare them as a man spares his son who serves him. Faithful Christian, be glad that you are found in His heavenly book of remembrance rather than simply in some earthly book. His book is what matters in the long run, indeed for eternity."

This book is dedicated to the many servants of the Lord who are unknown, unnoticed or forgotten by the twenty-first century Church. I could list some of the faculty from the schools mentioned above but most of them have received their reward and are now residing in heaven. I will be forever grateful to them for their patience with me and their input into my life. I am indebted to the one who has proofread this and other submitted manuscripts. I have learned a great deal from his keen insights and wisdom.

You may feel as though you are numbered with those of whom Paul wrote in I Corinthians 4:9-13 (NIV), "For it seems to me that God has put us apostles on display at the end of the procession, like those condemned to die in the arena. We have been made a spectacle to the whole universe, to angels as well as to human beings. We are fools for Christ, but you are so wise in Christ! We are weak, but you are strong! You are honored, we are dishonored! To this very hour we go hungry and thirsty, we are in rags, we are brutally treated, we are homeless. We work hard with our own hands. When we are cursed, we bless; when we are persecuted, we endure it; when we are slandered, we answer kindly. We have become the scum of the earth, the garbage of the world—right up to this moment." The MSG renders verse 13, "We're treated like garbage, potato peelings from the culture's kitchen." The Amplified Bible phrases verse 13, "When we are slandered and defamed, we [try to] answer softly and bring comfort. We have been made and are now the rubbish and filth of the world [the offscouring of all things, the scum of the earth]."

As faithful servants of the Lord, one's identity, confidence and contentment should be with those of whom it was said, Hebrews 11:32-38 (ESV), "And what more shall I say? For time would fail me to tell of Gideon, Barak, Samson, Jephthah, of David and Samuel and the prophets who through faith conquered kingdoms, enforced justice, obtained promises, stopped the mouths of lions, quenched the power of fire, escaped the edge of the sword, were made strong out of weakness, became mighty in war, put foreign armies to flight…Some were tortured, refusing to accept release, so that they might rise again to a better life. Others suffered mocking and flogging, and even chains and imprisonment. They were stoned, they were sawn in two, they were killed with the sword. They went about in skins of sheep and goats, destitute, afflicted, mistreated, of whom the world was not worthy—wandering about in deserts and mountains, and in dens and caves of the earth."

In many cases and situations, God's servants will be numbered with those "of whom the world was not worthy" and with those who feared the Lord and have their names inscribed in His "book of remembrance." In the story, A Christmas Carol by Charles Dickens, Tiny Tim is known for the statement: God bless Us, Every One! He cheerfully offers it as a blessing at Christmas dinner. As Dickens repeats this phrase at the end of his story, even so should the servants of God share these words with each other: "God bless us, every one!" One of the great truths I learned from the dedicated servants who served as faculty, instructors and friends is:

Do all things without grumbling or disputing; so that you will prove yourselves to be blameless and innocent, children of God above reproach in the midst of a crooked and perverse generation, among whom you appear as lights in the world, holding fast the word of life.
Philippians 2:14-16 (NASB)

Whether, then, you eat or drink or whatever you do, do all to the glory of God.
I Corinthians 10:31 (NASB)

Preface

When I began writing this book, the first title I had in mind was The Church and Culture: and A Quo Vadis (A Latin phrase meaning: whither goest thou/where are you going) reflection. As is common in writing, a different theme developed and the ideas were focused on the *Twenty-First Century Church: Is It Waxing of Waning?* Since writing the Book, I came across the following paragraphs (Source Unknown- probably from Pew Research)) that allows for a broader perspective. The question pursed was:

> Can the American Church be revitalized in the 21st Century? What's happening in the global church today? The religious landscape is particularly changing for the world's Christians. A century ago, 80 percent lived in North America and Europe, compared with just 40 percent today. In 1980, more Christians were found in the global South than the North for the first time in 1,000 years. Today, the Christian community in Latin America and Africa, alone, account for 1 billion people. Over the past 100 years, Christians grew from less than 10 percent of Africa's population to its nearly 500 million today. One out of four Christians in the world presently is an Africa, and the Pew Research Center estimates that will grow to 40 percent by 2030. Asia is also experiencing growth as world Christianity's center has moved not only South, but also East. In the last century, Christianity grew at twice the rate of population in that continent. Will America seek Jehovah God and remember...repent...return to Him? You, the reader, can make a difference in this crucial time!

The perspective and question deserves and requires consideration and response. There is no need for the Church in the United States to be ineffective. The burden and heart cry of the prophet Jeremiah was expressed time and time again. He first brings the message of the Lord with these words (Jeremiah 7:3-7, ESV).

> Thus says the LORD of hosts, the God of Israel: Amend your ways and your deeds, and I will let you dwell in this place. Do not trust in these deceptive words: This is the temple of the LORD, the temple of the LORD, the temple of the LORD. For if you truly amend your ways and your deeds, if you truly execute justice one with another, if you do not oppress the sojourner, the fatherless, or the widow, or shed innocent blood in this place, and if you do not go after other gods to your own harm, then I will let you dwell in this place, in the land that I gave of old to your fathers forever.

In a very succinct way, the prophet has made known the focus and scope of the church that purposes to obey the Lord.

The British Dictionary (dictionary.com) has the clear import of amend: "to improve; change for the better; to remove faults from; correct." There is nothing ambiguous of this message from the Lord by his prophet Jeremiah. The people and their leaders had become so set in their ways that they were recalcitrant (resisting authority and control; not obedient or compliant; hard to deal with). We have a glimpse of this response to the message from the Lord. It is stated in Jeremiah 18:11-12 (ESV):

> Now, therefore, say to the men of Judah and the inhabitants of Jerusalem: Thus says the LORD, Behold, I am shaping disaster against you and devising a plan against you. Return, everyone from his evil way, and amend your ways and your deeds. But they say, That is in

vain! We will follow our own plans, and will every one act according to the stubbornness of his evil heart.

There was a deep-seated rebellion and stubbornness that caused the people to believe the plan that men had devised was preferable to the ordained plan of God. This same issue is addressed once again in Jeremiah 26:12-13 (ESV):

> Then Jeremiah spoke to all the officials and all the people, saying, The LORD sent me to prophesy against this house and this city all the words you have heard. Now therefore amend your ways and your deeds, and obey the voice of the LORD your God, and the LORD will relent of the disaster that he has pronounced against you.

The indictment of God is then issued one additional time. It is a final opportunity for the people and their leaders to repent and return to the Lord. How will they respond when they hear the words of Jeremiah 35:12-15 (ESV)? With set minds, hardened hearts and seared consciences, the words from the Lord will fall upon deaf ears: "Then the word of the LORD came to Jeremiah: Thus says the LORD of hosts, the God of Israel: Go and say to the people of Judah and the inhabitants of Jerusalem, Will you not receive instruction and listen to my words? declares the LORD…I have spoken to you persistently, but you have not listened to me. I have sent to you all my servants the prophets, sending them persistently, saying, Turn now every one of you from his evil way, and amend your deeds, and do not go after other gods to serve them, and then you shall dwell in the land that I gave to you and your fathers. But you did not incline your ear or listen to me." One can sense the sorrow in the heart of God as this indictment is stated. It is not surprising that Jeremiah would weep because the people were rejecting the message from the Lord. They had opportunity to avoid the chaos and disaster but stubbornly refused the word of the Lord given by His servant Jeremiah.

The question regarding the Twenty-First Century Church in the United States is: Is the Church following the ways and words of the Lord or are men controlling the church and devising their plans rather than God's ordained plan for His people? If the Lord walked in the midst of the Twenty-First Century Church in the United States of America and assessed what it was doing, would he send His prophets with words similar to those delivered by Jeremiah? The church has been impacted by the culture and is too willing to be accommodating so that no one will be offended by the message or posture of the church. One of the sad moments for a cross section of Christendom today is the discussion and debate on whether or not it should pursue a progressive posture and ministry or continue with a traditional church concept. If the progressives choose to abort some of the long-held foundational principles and values to allow reception and audience with the evolving cultural norm, it will drift toward men devising their plans for God's church.

The Church does not have to allow itself to die. The message of the Lord by Jeremiah made that point over and over again. Another prophet also challenged a nation when he proclaimed in the name of the Lord, Ezekiel 18:31 (ESV), "Cast away from you all the transgressions that you have committed, and make yourselves a new heart and a new spirit! Why will you die, O house of Israel?" This message was echoed once again in Ezekiel 33:11 (ESV), "Say to them, As I live, declares the Lord GOD, I have no pleasure in the death of the wicked, but that the wicked turn from his way and live; turn back, turn back from your evil ways, for why will you die, O house of Israel?" I suspect that the Lord has not yet given up on the church in the United States of America. However, the time is growing shorter and the patience of God will not last too much longer. If the church will remember from where they have fallen, repent of their sins and transgressions and return to the Lord, His remedy will take place.

In Jeremiah 15:19-21 (ESV), we read: "Therefore thus says the LORD: If you return, I will restore you, and you shall stand before me. If you utter what is precious, and not what is worthless, you shall be as my mouth. They shall turn to you, but you shall not turn to them. And I will make you to this people a fortified wall of bronze; they will fight against you, but they shall not prevail over you, for I am with you to save you and deliver you, declares the LORD. I will deliver you out of the hand of the wicked, and redeem you from the grasp of the ruthless." Are you ready to receive and believe the words from the Lord? If so, the words of verse 19 are clear, forthright and unequivocal: "If you return, I will restore you, and you shall stand before me." This is the message the church needs to embrace. This is the affirmative action that will please the Lord. This will be the resultant blessing for all those who will seek after the ways of Almighty God rather than that which is devised as an alternative by men.

May the Lord enrich you with understanding, acceptance of His truth and blessing as you read this book! To God be the glory for the great things He will continually do in and through you. Follow and love Him with all your heart, soul, strength and mind.

Table of Contents

1. Vague Visualization 1
2. Spoken About or Being Done 13
3. Status Quo is Unacceptable 23
4. Form and Function 37
5. Highway of Holiness 47
6. Highway of Perfection 59
7. Highway of Carnality 71
8. Reclamation and Revitalization 81
9. Calamity of Carnality 93
10. Escaping the Grip of Carnality 107
11. Enculturated or Enraptured? 119
12. Constructing Crafty Narratives 131
13. Analysis and Determination 143
14. Fidelity or Falderal 155
15. Defining Thoughts 165
16. Authoritarian Domination 175
17. An Accurate Epitaph 187
18. Reasonable Alternative 197

1. Vague Visualization

And I tell you...I will build my church, and the gates of hell shall not prevail against it.
Matthew 16:18 (ESV)

The organized Church today should be an accurate and true representation of the Church Jesus Christ is in the process of building. It is also referred to as the invisible Church and the Bride of Christ. A valid consideration pertains to when the invisible Church fails to be seen in the visible Church. One can travel into almost any town or city in this country and see a multitude of Churches with chosen identities, such as Baptist, Presbyterian, Methodist and a host of other groups declaring themselves as being a Church. There are obvious distinctions. There are different denominations and affiliations. There are also doctrinal distinctions that separate groups from another, such as Reformed, Calvinistic, Arminian, Evangelical, etc. As a result, there is an antagonism between groups and divisions that seem irreparable. Personalities that seem larger than life attempt to exert their will over that of others and sooner or later division occurs.

A valid question to ponder is: Why is the invisible Church failing to be visible? What factors are present that result in the diminishing effectiveness of the visible Church? Why is it experiencing declining attendance and membership? What is one's understanding of the Bride of Christ and how He wants His Bride to appear to others? At this present time, what would be your assessment of the Church of Jesus Christ? Would it be the invisible Church is the Bride of Christ that is made up of all who are true believers, those whose calling and election are sure (See: II Peter 1:10). The visible Church is made up of those who have joined a group that professes belief in Jesus Christ. How is the secular world and culture responding to the visible Church today? Are they drawn to it or repulsed by it? A self-evaluation by a visible Church might include the questions, "Where are you and where are we going, and what is being done in keeping with God's will and direction for His Church?" This is the twenty-first century moment in which the Church should ask and then answer the question: "Whither goest thou (Where are you going)?" Is the Church waxing or waning? Is it effectively representing the invisible Bride of Christ? Why are a growing number of people hesitant or not attracted to the visible Church today?

The secular media is unabashed when it comes to their assessment of the visible Church. *The American Thinker* for January 14, 2015 contains an article, "Christianity Is Losing in America" by Craig Dunkley. He writes:

> Christianity is under attack in America, and it's losing. Meanwhile, the Church is, in general, sitting out the fight and hoping the problem goes away. Hope is not a strategy. It is time to act. Since its inception, the United States has been a predominantly Christian nation…Our sense of personal freedom and tolerance, backed by a thoroughly Judeo-Christian worldview, has contributed mightily to this nation's greatness. That worldview, and the Christian faith behind it, is being whittled away by the media, our popular culture, and a newly emboldened 'activist atheist' movement. The pace of that whittling has accelerated over the last decade… .

In his paragraph, "Churches on the Sidelines" he comments: "It's important to note that Churches do fantastic work. Christian charities help people across the globe, Christian missionaries risk life and limb to spread the faith abroad, and Churches provide comfort and support to millions…If Christians do not answer the call now, then even more people will turn away from Christianity because they think it's not for

THE TWENTY-FIRST CENTURY CHURCH: IS IT WAXING OR WANING?

them...when it might be exactly what they're seeking in their lives."

The Huffington Post on November 17, 2014 contained a column by Steve McSwain (Speaker, Author, Counselor to Congregations, Ambassador to the Council on the Parliament for the World's Religions, and Spiritual Teacher). He wrote on the subject: Is the Church dying? He stated: "Given the widespread departure from the Church in all its varied expressions, it is a legitimate question. Add to this the reality that the Millennial generation has not only left the Church but does not seem to be returning and you have a recipe for disaster. In the last few years, we have heard much about the "Nones." These are those persons...who no longer identify with any particular religion. They are the religiously unaffiliated. Some of them, perhaps even the majority of them, were formerly religious. And, many of them still regard themselves as spiritual persons who simply no longer identify with any religious denomination (My own experience is that many of them have just left organized religion. Their faith is still meaningful to them, however. A few of them identify as agnostics or even atheists. And even that number is rapidly growing)." He continues his assessment: "The 'Dones' are the newest 'Nones'. Some of the American Church's most faithful and active members are becoming the quickest to permanently walk out the doors, according to new research...One writer who examined a growing population he calls The Dones, indicated they are a group of once-dedicated Church members who have decided to stop going to Church. For the visible Church, this phenomenon sets up a growing danger...The very people on whom a Church relies for lay leadership, service and financial support, are going away. And the problem is compounded by the fact that younger people in the next generation, the Millennials, are not lining up to refill the emptying pews...The Dones are fatigued with the Sunday routine of plop, pray and pay... According to the research, Church leaders have little chance of getting the Dones to return to Church…The Research suggests focusing on not losing these people in the first place."

What do people see as the reality of the visible Church today? What should an internal assessment of the visible Church entail and include? This author wrote and posted a Blog on January 13, 2015 entitled, "Conspicuous." Some of what was written and contained in the Blog included the following:

> Acts 28:25-28 closes with these words to a people who had numerous opportunities to hear and respond to God's Word and His apostles but chose to ignore them. Paul summarizes and made one declarative statement to and about them: The Holy Spirit was right in saying to your fathers through Isaiah the prophet: Go to this people and say, you will indeed hear but never understand, and you will indeed see but never perceive. For this people's heart has grown dull, and with their ears they can barely hear, and their eyes they have closed; lest they should see with their eyes and hear with their ears and understand with their heart and turn, and I would heal them.

A parallel for this passage is Revelation 2 and 3. Jesus walks in the midst of the Churches and makes His assessment and proclamation about and to them. To each Church, Jesus said: I know your works…I know all about you. The point was that nothing can be hidden from God. Jesus stated some Churches had done some very good things. The issue He raises is that they have missed that which is conspicuous to the observing eye, such as, departure from one's first love; allowing respect of persons to prevail; the toleration of error, blasphemy, and sin, etc. To those who chose to be oblivious to the conspicuous, the words of Jesus are consistent: Remember what you are supposed to be; Repent for what you have allowed yourself to become, and return to the core values and foundational principles from which you never should have

THE TWENTY-FIRST CENTURY CHURCH: IS IT WAXING OR WANING?

departed. For more than a generation, there has been the promotion and emphasis upon Church growth in most visible Church groups. Some denominations place emphasis on numbers to measure their growth. Attention is given to the new members joining, people being baptized, professions of faith, weekly attendance, increased offerings, etc. Despite the best efforts of the visible Church, much of the effort has been to no avail. Every year, hundreds of Churches are closing and people are departing from regular participation in the visible Church. A sad factor is that more Churches each year are being closed than started. The Church seems to be incapable to act in a way that would promote Church health rather than continuance with a Church malady. It should be a logical conclusion that Church health will always precede Church growth. There is only one way to achieve Church growth and that is according to God's methodology, precepts and standards.

Where can and should a Church begin to achieve both health and growth? One passage offering the remedy is Deuteronomy 10:12-16 (ESV): "And now, Israel, what does the Lord your God require of you, but to fear the Lord your God, to walk in all his ways, to love him, to serve the Lord your God with all your heart and with all your soul, and to keep the commandments and statutes of the Lord, which I am commanding you today for your good? Behold, to the Lord your God belong heaven and the heaven of heavens, the earth with all that is in it. Yet the Lord set his heart in love on your fathers and chose their offspring after them, you above all peoples, as you are this day. Circumcise therefore the foreskin of your heart, and be no longer stubborn." The visible Church must pursue being spiritually healthy before it exerts its energy to achieve Church growth. It is of no value or benefit for a visible Church to pretend it is healthy when it is sick and dying. It is similar to the condition of God's people when Isaiah was sent to them to give The Lord's assessment of their true condition: "Ah, sinful nation, a people laden with iniquity, offspring of evildoers, children who deal corruptly! They have forsaken the Lord, they have despised the Holy One of Israel, they are utterly estranged. Why will you still be struck down? Why will you continue to rebel? The whole head is sick, and the whole heart faint. From the sole of the foot even to the head, there is no soundness in it, but bruises and sores and raw wounds; they are not pressed out or bound up or softened with oil..." (Isaiah 1:4-6, ESV).

Is the visible Church a true reflection of the invisible Church, the Bride of Jesus Christ? If not, why not? What is the task, ministry, mission and vision of the visible Church today? If most Church members were asked to articulate why they were attending a particular visible Church, would their answer have anything to do with the task, ministry, mission and vision for the Church? At the very least, the Church leadership and members should be able to articulate that it is to stand in the cultural gap and proclaim the Gospel of the Lord Jesus Christ. It would involve a united effort and participation to extend oneself beyond all comfort zones and to reach out to those who are included in the "whosoever" spoken of in the Gospel (John 3:16) and included with those who can call on the name of the Lord to be saved (Romans 10:13). The strategy must be more than newspaper advertisements and posters inviting the public to "come to us." Obviously, that hasn't been working very well and very few, if any, are coming. The commitment must be present that the visible Church will "go to them" and to seek those who need to be reached for the Bride-groom, Jesus Christ. In the "Parable of The Great Banquet" (Luke 14:12-24), the master of the house sends out his servants to invite guests to his banquet table. The servants report that they have tried but the response has been minimal. The master then indicates they are to keep trying and to do so with greater urgency. The words of urgency are (Vs. 23): "Go out into the highways and along the hedges, and compel them to come in, so that my house may be filled." This is the task of the visible Church today? Is your Church doing it or is it easier to make excuses to the master regarding why there is still room at the banquet table? There needs to be

THE TWENTY-FIRST CENTURY CHURCH: IS IT WAXING OR WANING?

the readiness and willingness to regularly and consistently go and present The Master's invitation to come to Him and His banquet table. It must be noticed that there is to be no limitation on who is to be contacted and invited; no one is to be bypassed or deemed to be unlikely; no one should be viewed as inconsequential; no one should be viewed as being insignificant; and we should determine that no one is avoided because they are considered to be not our kind of people.

There are many Churches that are at a crisis moment and threshold. Despite their determination to keep on keeping on, they are in a slow, torturous process of dying. In some instances, they may already have died and are reluctant to admit it. They need to assess and determine where they are going and what they are doing in terms of viable ministry. There is no purpose in continuing as a dying entity while avoiding the prescription that can result in revitalization and new-found good health. Can a sick Church be revitalized and become healthy once again? How can a visible Church move from obvious failure to success? The following was an entry in *This Day In Presbyterian History*, January 8, 2015. The theme is: Prestigious Congregation Votes into the Presbyterian Church in America (January 8, 1978). A question for consideration is: How or when did it become a prestigious congregation. The pastor of the group had been called by 47 people in 1959 to develop a Church plant opportunity. At the time, they were meeting in an elementary school cafeteria. After being there for a year and faithfully preaching and teaching this group, the attendance changed dramatically. The group of 47 diminished to just 17 people. Can this apparent failure be reversed and become a success? If the pastor and group continued doing what it had been doing the demise would cause an obvious result and the decision would be to cease and desist from continuing on. At this discouraging moment, the pastor received an invitation to conduct an evangelistic series at two rural Churches in Georgia. When he arrived there, the rural pastor informed him that he would not only be proclaiming the

Word but that he would also be expected to go door to door in the area to personally present the gospel to the unChurched and unsaved. The visiting evangelist had not planned on this aspect of ministry and was not very capable at doing it. What does an evangelist do when pressed into a one on one personal presentation of the gospel?

The evangelist bungled his attempt at the first home visited. The rural pastor took over the task and proceeded to lead the person to making a profession of faith. It was not just in this one home. The rural pastor was enabled to lead soul after soul to Jesus Christ. What made the difference? Why was the rural pastor able to do what the Evangelist was unable to do? The above referenced website records the following: "What he (the evangelist) didn't know at the time was that the two rural congregations had prayed for the salvation of specific people for two years. Further, just prior to the evangelistic meetings, a young banker had dropped dead. That fact, plus the prayers, made the diagnostic question which began with "Suppose you were to die today," suddenly real to every citizen in the area." The evangelist would return to his young and dying group of 17 with a new vision and emphasis in soul-winning. He would expand on the presentation of the rural pastor's question with two questions of his own: "Suppose you were to die today, do you know for certain you would go to heaven?" The second question was: "Suppose you did die today and you were to stand in the presence of God and He said to you, why should I let you into My Heaven, what would you say?" Was this new vision and emphasis effective? Was there any tangible evidence that concerted prayer for specific individuals and the presentation of the gospel to them would bring about positive result? When the Coral Ridge Presbyterian Church affiliated with a newly formed denomination in 1973, the Presbyterian Church in America, the group had grown from 17 people to more than 8,000 members.

Can this type of effective impact occur in a rural Church setting today? Can it occur where your Church is located? One of the basic components for the effectiveness of such an effort

THE TWENTY-FIRST CENTURY CHURCH: IS IT WAXING OR WANING?

is a consecrated group of God's people committed to united and specific prayer for the unsaved (lost) in the community and area. After earnestly praying specifically, the commitment will include a readiness and willingness to go to those for whom prayer was offered and present the Gospel to those residing there. To begin doing this work of ministry, one would do well to commit to memory some Scripture verses that will be vital to the presentation of the Gospel. An easy method is using The Roman Road to Salvation. It is usually presented in five steps (although some adapted it to include additional steps. It is appropriate to ask if a person has a Bible of their own. You will want them to see the truths you will present to them in their own Bible. Assist them in finding the Book of Romans before you begin your presentation of the Gospel. Then begin the basic presentation in the following manner:

> 1. Everyone needs salvation because all of us have sinned. Use Romans 3:23 (you can also use Romans 3:10-12 to indicate that no one is righteous).
> 2. The price or consequence for sin is death. Use Romans 6:23(a).
> 3. Jesus Christ died for our sins and the free gift for us is eternal life in Jesus Christ. Use Romans 6:23(b). You can also use Romans 5:8 to emphasize God's great love for us in that while we were still sinners (or sinning) Christ died for us.
> 4. In order to receive this gift of God's love and grace, one must confess that Jesus Christ is Lord and must believe that God raised Him from the dead. Use all of Romans 10:9-10. When this is done, Romans 10:13 becomes one's reality, "Whoever calls on the name of the Lord shall be saved."
> 5. Receiving God's gift of salvation also results in one's peace with God. Use Romans 5:1. Furthermore, eternal life in Christ means that there is no condemnation

because we now belong to Jesus Christ. Use Romans 8:1. The assurance we now have in Christ Jesus is that no one and no thing can ever separate us from God. Use Romans 8:38-39.

You will need to be prepared to lead a person to pray to receive Jesus Christ as one's personal Savior. An idea of such a prayer is: "Dear Jesus, I admit that I am a sinner. I have done many things that haven't pleased You. I have been living my life for myself and my pleasures. I'm sorry for ignoring You and Your Word for so long. I repent and ask you to forgive me of all my sins and trespasses. I believe that You died on the cross to save me. I want to surrender my life to You and Your will for me. Help me to live for You from this moment and for the rest of my life. I ask this in Jesus name. Amen!" After the prayer is concluded, you should extend your right hand and say words to the effect: "Let me be the first to welcome you into the family of God!" This is the work, ministry and commitment that will cause the visible Church to flourish once again and be a true representation of the invisible Church. The Bride of Christ cannot afford the luxury of business as usual. The Church cannot have an effective and triumphant ministry while it is staggering in self-indulgence and self-interests. The Church will not be seen as a viable alternative when it is lacking vision or a sense of mission. The Church in this state and condition becomes an exhibit of the invisible Church failing to be visible. It demonstrates it is waning rather than waxing. The Church must come in repentance before God and pray…

Just as I am—without one plea,
But that Thy blood was shed for me,
And that Thou bidst me come to Thee—
O Lamb of God, I come, I come.

Just as I am—and waiting not
To rid my soul of one dark blot,

THE TWENTY-FIRST CENTURY CHURCH:
IS IT WAXING OR WANING?

To Thee whose blood can cleanse each spot—
O Lamb of God, I come, I come.

Just as I am—though tossed about
With many a conflict, many a doubt,
Fightings and fears within, without—
O Lamb of God, I come, I come.

Just as I am—poor, wretched, blind;
Sight, riches, healing of the mind,
Yea, all I need in Thee to find—
O Lamb of God, I come, I come.

Just as I am—Thy love unknown
Hath broken every barrier down;
Now, to be Thine, yea, Thine alone—
O Lamb of God, I come, I come.

(Public Domain - Words By: Charlotte Elliot, 1835)

2. Spoken About or Being Done

The fruit of the righteous is a tree of life, and he who is wise wins souls.
Proverbs 11:30 (KJV)

The previous chapter used an illustration to state that failure does not need to be final. The Church that began with 47 people and shrank to 17 within its first year recovered and expanded its ministry when evangelism became a central part of who they were and would become by God's grace. The rural Pastor had learned that when specific and persistent prayer was offered regarding the unChurched and unsaved it would be honored by God as follow-up visitation evangelism took place. There is also an interesting observation made about R.B. Kuiper, January 31, 2015 (*http://www.thisday.pcahistory.org*): "Among that broad span of the whole counsel of God, and one which seminary professors and students often fail, is the area of Reformed evangelism. Listen to his words in his book, *To Be Or Not to Be Reformed*." He wrote: "God forbid that we should become complacent about our progress in evangelism! Our zeal for evangelism is not nearly as warm as it ought to be. Our evangelistic labors are not nearly as abundant as they should be. Our prayers for the translation of souls from darkness into God's marvelous light must become far more fervent (p. 77). What R. B. Kuiper wrote fifty years ago is true in our day. Ask yourselves the question, "Am I a zealous evangelist?"

As we ponder the question about being a zealous evangelist, we should also consider these probing words of The Reverend William E. Hill. He was for many years a distinguished pastor in Hopewell, Virginia, leaving that post to become the founder of the Presbyterian Evangelistic Fellowship, a work which continues to this day. Moreover, he was prominent among the founding fathers of the PCA (Presbyterian Church In America), working faithfully to steer a true course for the new denomination. At the fourth PCA General Assembly in 1976, he was the keynote speaker. Part of what he observed and stated was:

> Looking at the situation after our third General Assembly, we raise the question: Does the PCA need revival? Some may say: That is a silly question—we are already in revival. This I question. Some may suggest that we need doctrinal instruction. Others may say we need to perfect our organization and outreach. It seems to me, however, that what is most desperately needed in the PCA is real revival. Of doctrinal identification we have enough. Of ecclesiastical machinery we have too much. Of debating fine points we are weary. Now the question is or should be: How in the world are we going to meet the needs of many of our small, struggling groups? This is a big question. Indeed, how are we going to find ministers to pastor these people? Another big question. The answer to all these questions, I believe, is revival. Without it we will degenerate into an ecclesiastical machine, grinding out materials, spewing forth pronouncements, fussing over theological distinctions, and languishing in barrenness and sterility. If we had a real filling of the Spirit, would there not be men among us evidently "full of the Spirit" and would there not be more talk about it? Is the reason, possibly, that we need real revival to create within us a deeper spiritual discernment, spiritual expectation, zeal, eagerness, and effectiveness in witness? We need revival because truly spiritual Churches should grow by making converts, not just by accepting transfers. We have seen Churches springing up. We have seen Churches growing. But we've seen mighty little of growth by conversions. Just

THE TWENTY-FIRST CENTURY CHURCH: IS IT WAXING OR WANING?

by looking at the figures for 1974 on additions by profession, one can tell that our Churches are not growing by the method God ordained by which Churches should primarily grow: The Lord added to the Church daily such as should be saved (Acts 2:47). Additions to our Churches have not been, for the most part, by conversion. We need the kind of revival that will bring people in great numbers to the Lord Jesus Christ and we need Churches that grow by converting. A few Churches here and there are exceptions; they do grow primarily by converting, but possibly you could name them on the fingers of one hand.

The words he spoke are almost prophetic. It is sad to see Churches that have remained small, struggling to survive and shrinking steadily. Despite the fact that there has been a steady production of evangelistic tools and methods, they are not often utilized. For many years, tools and booklets such as *Steps To Peace with God* (Billy Graham Evangelistic Association); *The Bridge* (The Navigators); *The Four Spiritual Laws* (Campus Crusade for Christ - now CRU); *The Roman Road to Salvation* (Five Steps within the Book of Romans - indicated earlier); and *Evangelism Explosion* (written by D. James Kennedy) have been available as an aid. The booklets contained a brief presentation of the Gospel. When used door to door, the approach was: "Have you heard of (name of the evangelistic tool being used)?" Most people would respond with: No! The next step would be to hand them a copy of the booklet being utilized and then say: I would like to read it with you. It will take about three minutes of your time. Then - without hesitancy one should proceed with the reading. If the person refuses the approach and becomes rude, be kind and gentle toward them. As you begin to leave, encourage them to read the booklet when they have time to do so.

It is vital to make note of the residence visited and the response of the person. The purpose is to follow up that visit with specific and persistent prayer for the individual or household. The prayer should be based upon the words of Scripture:

> For as the rain and the snow come down from heaven, And do not return there without watering the earth And making it bear and sprout, And furnishing seed to the sower and bread to the eater; So will My word be which goes forth from My mouth; It will not return to Me empty, Without accomplishing what I desire, And without succeeding in the matter for which I sent it (Isaiah 55:10-11, NASB).

One can never determine how God will work in the heart and life of the one who was contacted. The focus of the one who speaks the gospel to another individual is not on the immediate response of the person contacted.

There was a man who was nearing death who had little use for the Church and most who call themselves Christian. His wife was concerned for her dying husband and wanted someone to share the gospel with her husband. Knowing that he was enduring discomfort and that the visit would have to be brief, the booklet: *Steps To Peace With God* was used. It was shared and left with him. When the maid had come in to tidy the house and the area around his bed, the booklet could no longer be located. The man asked his wife what had happened to it because he wanted to read it again. She called the man (a pastor who her husband liked) who had left it with him and he immediately returned to the home with another copy. It gave another opportunity to share the gospel and to pray with him once again. While there was no audible response given to the Pastor, a relative would later claim that he had led her husband to a saving knowledge of the Lord Jesus Christ. An important fact to remember that it is not the one who gets the credit or who claims the result that matters but the work that God has done in the heart and soul of the person who was so close to entering eternity. The principle is that one plants, another waters and God gives the increase (See: I Corinthians 3:7).

One's confidence should be based upon the fact that God's Word being used in God's way will always bring about God's desired result. In his attempt to prevent sectarianism in the Church as it was being established, the Apostle Paul was careful to state in I Corinthians 3:5-11 (NLT),

> After all, who is Apollos? Who is Paul? We are only God's servants through whom you believed the good news. Each of us did the work the Lord gave us. I planted the seed in your hearts, and Apollos watered it, but it was God who made it grow. It's not important who does the planting, or who does the watering. What's important is that God makes the seed grow.

The important point being made is that each of us faithfully did the work the Lord gave us to do. The unwavering point is that the distinction is made regarding what is being spoken about versus that which is being done. It is important to note this because the emphasis should never be on who is involved in doing the task but rather what the true motivation and goal is as the task is being done. Person A may be the person God wants to be a seed-sower. Person B may be the person God wants to be in charge of the garden hose or watering can. Each person is to do the work the Lord has given each one to do.

A major hurdle one has to face is the fear factor in doing the Lord's work and the given assignment. In many different circumstances and situations, the Scriptures utilize the words: "Do not fear." The propensity of many people is to have a fear (anxiety) regarding the unknown. In walking up to a home where inhabitants are unknown, the hesitancy is caused by the unknown fear rather than the infused courage which should be dominant in our lives. What was it that Joshua needed the most as he faced the unknown dangers and challenges as he moved forward to do that which God wanted him to do? In Joshua 1:5-9 (ESV, selected), we read:

> I will be with you. I will not leave you or forsake you. Be strong and courageous…Only be strong and very courageous, being careful to do according to all the law that Moses my servant commanded you. Do not turn from it to the right hand or to the left, that you may have good success wherever you go. This Book of the Law shall not depart from your mouth, but you shall meditate on it day and night, so that you may be careful to do according to all that is written in it. For then you will make your way prosperous, and then you will have good success. Have I not commanded you? Be strong and courageous. Do not be frightened, and do not be dismayed, for the Lord your God is with you wherever you go.

Since the Lord has promised to be with His servants wherever they are sent, one should set aside all fears and anxieties and learn to lean fully upon the Lord and His sustaining strength.

Questions: Do you believe the principle and promise given by the Lord to Joshua is valid and applicable for you today? Is there any time-frame or limitation placed upon the word spoken by the Lord to His faithful servant? Has the Lord changed in any way from the day of Joshua to the current time? When the Apostle Paul had entered Corinth, it was a place of considerable sinning and many challenges. It was not a religious community or a place that one would deem to be a place for effective evangelism. There are many cities, towns and communities in the United States where that analysis would also be applicable. What should a person do when considering where one's energy and effort should be exerted and be most fruitful? There is a lesson one can learn about action and reaction in Acts

18. In verses 4-6, we learn what Paul did, how the people responded and how Paul reacted to that response. We note:

> Every Sabbath he reasoned in the synagogue, trying to persuade Jews and Greeks. When Silas and Timothy came from Macedonia, Paul devoted himself exclusively to preaching, testifying to the Jews that Jesus was the Messiah. But when they opposed Paul and became abusive, he shook out his clothes in protest and said to them, Your blood be on your own heads! I am innocent of it. From now on I will go to the Gentiles.

In other words, Paul no longer believed it would do any good trying to persuade the religious elite and leadership in terms of the Gospel and the reality of who Jesus Christ was and did.

Questions: Did Paul have a right to react the way he did? Were the people rebelling against Paul, or the Messiah, or both? Had Paul responded with appealing or confrontational words? Had Paul consulted with the Lord in terms of his response and reaction? Had he given any consideration to God's will for a lost and rebellious people? Was his reaction due to his sense that it was a personal rejection of him? What was the Lord's response and reaction to the people who had responded so badly and negatively? In Acts 18:9-11, we understand the Lord's response and purpose being clarified for Paul. "One night the Lord spoke to Paul in a vision: Do not be afraid; keep on speaking, do not be silent. For I am with you, and no one is going to attack and harm you, because I have many people in this city. So Paul stayed in Corinth for a year and a half, teaching them the word of God." Should we not be encouraged by these words as we purpose to do God's work in the community and locale where He has placed us? Our answer should be an emphatic, Yes!

It is too easy for any of us to think we are unable, unequipped and ill-prepared to do any positive ministry for the Lord. One of the sad realities is that too many local Churches allow for classification of people groups within the Church. Those who are classified as being most prominent receive the greatest privilege while those who are deemed to be inconsequential or insignificant are tolerated but not fully embraced. In 2012, a book I wrote, *Realizing Significance*, was published. It is based upon the text in Mark 4:35-41.

> On the same day, when evening had come, He said to them, Let us cross over to the other side. Now when they had left the multitude, they took Him along in the boat as He was. And other little boats were also with Him. And a great windstorm arose, and the waves beat into the boat, so that it was already filling. But He was in the stern, asleep on a pillow. And they awoke Him and said to Him, Teacher, do You not care that we are perishing?

A point made in the book is about the one big boat where Jesus and the Disciples were and the other little boats where the people of lesser significance were following them. In the "Introduction," I wrote: "The question we all must consider and answer: If we were on the boat with Jesus, what would we have done and what would we have said to Him? Would we have awakened Him and said: We're not certain of our survival, but the other little boats with us are in more immediate danger, can You do something to keep them from perishing in the sea?" The book (recently edited and republished) states:

> There will always be the other little boats and those who are categorized as the little people or other sheep by those who are preoccupied with their own survival. What is often ignored and overlooked is that the little boats can be transformed into functional and useful vessels;

THE TWENTY-FIRST CENTURY CHURCH: IS IT WAXING OR WANING?

> the little people can be transformed into a consecrated people who are functional within the kingdom of God; and the other sheep can be redeemed and become a visible and viable part of the flock of God. The work God may do in their behalf is to transform them from dysfunction to function; from uselessness to usefulness; and from being purposeless to being purposeful all by His grace and in accordance with His will.

With this in mind, as we consider and commit to the ministry of evangelism, we must remember and be concerned about the other little boats and those who are viewed as little people, those whom Jesus sought who are the other sheep. These who are of little or no consequence in the eyes of the ones who spend too much time focused upon themselves, are equally precious in the sight of God. Note these excerpts from Isaiah 43:1-4.

> Fear not, for I have redeemed you; I have called you by name, you are mine. When you pass through the waters, I will be with you; and through the rivers, they shall not overwhelm you…Because you are precious in my eyes, and honored, and I love you…

Despite the presence of those who are deemed the elite or more important, those who have or display very little time, if any at all, for little boats, little people or other sheep, and for those who are barely surviving and falling through the cracks of our culture, let it be remembered that you are loved by God, redeemed by Him and are precious to Him and in His sight.

A man who was viewed as a philosopher, theologian and apologist was Francis Schaeffer. Even though he was a person of stature, he was always very practical in his ministry. No one was deemed to be inconsequential or insignificant. In 1974, he

James Perry

authored a Book titled, *No Little People*. A brief summary shares the heart of this man and his ministry focus.

> The Scripture emphasizes that much can come from little if the little is truly consecrated to God. There are no little people and no big people in the true spiritual sense, but only consecrated and unconsecrated people. We must remember throughout our lives that in God's sight there are no little people and no little places. Only one thing is important: to be consecrated persons in God's place for us, at each moment.

His shared thoughts reminded me of the chorus:

> *Every moment of the day, My Father cares for me.*
> *Every moment of the day, My heart from fear is free.*
> *He Who sees the sparrows fall Will hear my call*
> *Every moment of the day My Father watches over me.*
> *(Chorus - Author Unknown)*

3. Status Quo is Unacceptable

> *Go to the ant, you sluggard; consider its ways and be wise! It has no commander, no overseer or ruler, yet it stores its provisions in summer and gathers its food at harvest. How long will you lie there, you sluggard? When will you get up from your sleep? A little sleep, a little slumber, a little folding of the hands to rest—and poverty will come on you like a thief and scarcity like an armed man.*
> *Proverbs 6:8-11 (NIV)*

The last chapter concluded with reference to those who are classified as little people. The point underscored by Francis Schaeffer was: "There are no little people and no big people. There are only consecrated people or unconsecrated people." Another application that can be made is that God enables the willing and consecrated person to do great things for Him. The greater issue is whether or not there are people willing to do the task of evangelism within the visible Church. If one ever wonders about the Christian influence being diminished within our culture, there should be an assessment made in terms of whether or not the invisible Church (the Bride of Jesus Christ) is viable and visible within your sphere of the culture. Part of what will be observed is in terms of how seriously you are taking a serious God. Another important truth one should always remember is that we are not called to be like other Christians, because we are called to be like Jesus Christ. The summation of who we are is given in I Peter 2:8-9.

> But you are a chosen race, a royal priesthood, a holy nation, a people for his own possession, that you may proclaim the excellencies of him who called you out of darkness into his marvelous light. Once you were not a people, but now you are God's people; once you had not

received mercy, but now you have received mercy.

In some translations, the phrase "a people for His own possession" has been translated "a peculiar people." That idea should only suggest that we are uniquely chosen by the Lord to be His people and to do His work in His way.

Some questions that need review and response include: Are you content with the status quo in your life, spiritual values you seek to incorporate into your life and the visible Church you attend? Are you willing to make a deliberate and determined effort to touch the lives of others in your community and culture for Jesus Christ? Are you ready to be involved in an operation rescue as you endeavor to assist and care for the other little boats struggling on the stormy sea; the little people that go unnoticed and uncared for; and the other sheep who are deemed to be of little consequence, significance or value?

There is an interesting historical record of the role that little boats can accomplish when attached to and joined by other little boats. The scene is The Battle of Dunkirk during World War II. *Wikipedia* (and other sources indicate the following):

> In May 1940, during the Battle of France, the British Expeditionary Force in France aiding the French, was cut off from the rest of the French Army by the German advance. Encircled by the Germans they retreated to the area around the port of Dunkirk. The German land forces could have easily destroyed the British Expeditionary Force, especially when many of the British troops, in their haste to withdraw, had left behind their heavy equipment. For years, it was assumed that Adolf Hitler ordered the German Army to stop the attack, favoring bombardment by the Luftwaffe. However, according to the Official War Diary of Army Group A, its commander, General Oberst Gerd von Rundstedt, ordered the halt. Hitler merely validated the order several hours after the fact. This lull in the action gave the

THE TWENTY-FIRST CENTURY CHURCH: IS IT WAXING OR WANING?

British a few days to evacuate by sea. Winston Churchill, Prime Minister of England, ordered any ship or boat available, large or small, to pick up the stranded soldiers at Dunkirk. It took over 900 vessels (many of them little Boats) to evacuate the Allied forces and 338,226 men were evacuated and rescued. Churchill would refer to it as the miracle of Dunkirk.

Some of the things that made an important difference for those running the risks and dangers with their vessels was the compelling demand of Winston Churchill, the enormous numbers of allied forces in imminent danger and the immediacy of the decision required to act now. There was no room for complacency or rationalization. There was no room for any excuse or delay. Any refusal could cause the death of the embattled and trapped troops at Dunkirk.

One is reminded of the occasion when Jesus Christ was summoning different ones to follow Him. In a previous chapter, reference was made to the parable of the great banquet in Luke 14. In verse 15-21 (ESV), the following is recorded:

> When one of those who reclined at table with him heard these things, he said to him, Blessed is everyone who will eat bread in the kingdom of God! But he said to him, A man once gave a great banquet and invited many. And at the time for the banquet he sent his servant to say to those who had been invited, Come, for everything is now ready. But they all alike began to make excuses. The first said to him, I have bought a field, and I must go out and see it. Please have me excused. And another said, I have bought five yoke of oxen, and I go to examine them. Please have me excused. And another said, I have married a wife, and therefore I cannot come. So the servant came and reported these things to his master. Then the master of the house became angry.

The online dictionary *(dictionary.com)* lists several possible definitions for the word excuse. Among the possibilities for the above reference in Luke 14, the most applicable are: "to release from an obligation or duty; to seek or obtain exemption or release for oneself." *Barnes Notes on Luke* states the following (Luke 14:18-20):

> And they all with one consent began to make excuse. The first said unto him, I have bought a piece of ground, and I must needs go and see it: I pray thee have me excused…Perhaps he had purchased it on condition that he found it as good as it had been represented to him. I must needs go - I have necessity, or am obliged to go and see it; possibly pleading a contract or an agreement that he would go soon and examine it. However, we may learn from this that sinners sometimes plead that they are under a necessity to neglect the affairs of religion. The affairs of the world, they pretend, are so pressing that they cannot find time to attend to their souls. They have no time to pray, or read the Scriptures, or keep up the worship of God. In this way many lose their souls. God cannot regard such an excuse for neglecting religion with approbation. He commands us to seek 'first' the kingdom of God and his righteousness, nor can He approve any excuse that people may make for not doing it.

It is strange how the tangible things of life that entail a financial consideration override and are allowed to supersede spiritual considerations. *Barnes Notes on Luke* further explains the Luke text.

> Another said, I have bought five yoke of oxen, and I go to prove them: I pray thee have me excused. To try them, to see if he had made a good bargain. It is worthy of remark that this excuse was very trifling. He could as

easily have tried them at any other time as then, and his whole conduct shows that he was more disposed to gratify himself than to accept the invitation of his friend. He was selfish; just as all sinners are, who, to gratify their own worldliness and sins, refuse to accept the offers of the gospel.

Personal preferences and self-satisfying involvements allow one to ignore a gracious and important invitation to attend and sit at the table of the Master. It exhibits indifference and disregard to respond affirmatively to a gracious invitation.

Barnes Notes on Luke observes, "Another said, I have married a wife, and therefore I cannot come. Our Savior here doubtless intends to teach us that the love of earthly relatives and friends often takes off the affections from God, and prevents our accepting the blessings which he would bestow on us. This was the most trifling excuse of all; and we cannot but be amazed that such excuses are suffered to interfere with our salvation, and that people can be satisfied for such reasons to exclude themselves from the kingdom of God." The wise person might ask whether or not the invitation would include his bride. The request wasn't made because of his overriding physical relationship that left him, in his thinking, no room for consideration of anything that would detract his plans and his new personal relationship.

How does God view His provision and the responses it receives from people today? Romans 1:18-20 (ESV) states one of God's responses: "For the wrath of God is revealed from heaven against all ungodliness and unrighteousness of men, who by their unrighteousness suppress the truth. For what can be known about God is plain to them, because God has shown it to them. For his invisible attributes, namely, his eternal power and divine nature, have been clearly perceived, ever since the creation of the world, in the things that have been made. So they are without excuse." The last phrase is God's indictment, "So they are without excuse." In other words, there is no acceptable excuse or alternative to the invitation of the Master. A person may rationalize or deny the existence of God and the necessity of complying with His invitations. Anyone choosing this response, supposing that is feasible, does so at his own eternal peril.

We need to direct our thoughts to those who are mentioned as servants to the Master. The servants have been given an instruction and are under obligation to respond affirmatively to it. It is not up to the servant to rationalize or determine the time-frame for extending the invitation of the Master. The Master uses a tone of urgency in the assignment and the invitation to be extended. Within the Church today, the servants offer as many excuses regarding their obligation to extend the invitation as the ones to whom it is to be presented. All one needs to do is to look and observe the empty pews in the Church they attend. This fact screams out to us that there is plenty of room to accommodate more guests so that the Master's House will be filled. Regardless of what people in the Church may say, it is obvious they are satisfied with the status quo. Things remain just as they are and have become. While there may be a voiced hope that things will change and that the Church will grow, very little is done to accomplish the voiced hope. There is little thought given to the condition of a Church's declining health and the need to assistance to bring about possible remedy. If this was happening physically to oneself or loved one, with a great sense of urgency and immediacy, an Emergency Medical Technician (EMT) would be summoned to resuscitate or to stabilize the one impacted physically. There seems to be very little concern for the Church or Churches that are gasping their last breath. The demographics in many areas have shifted and developing a cross-cultural ministry could be the reasonable alternative but little or no consideration is given to that type of vision or outreach.

The *European Leadership Forum Newsletter* for February 2015 includes a Lecture: "Why Is Today's Church Being Molded

THE TWENTY-FIRST CENTURY CHURCH: IS IT WAXING OR WANING?

By The Culture?" It is written by Bruce Little and raises a probing consideration, "Numerous Christian authors are now asking why many evangelical Churches in the West look so much like the world contrary to the command of Romans 12:1-2." These verses state clearly and concisely one of the basic principles for the follower of Jesus Christ.

> I urge you, brethren, by the mercies of God, to present your bodies a living and holy sacrifice, acceptable to God, which is your spiritual service of worship. And do not be conformed to this world, but be transformed by the renewing of your mind, so that you may prove what the will of God is, that which is good and acceptable and perfect. For through the grace given to me I say to everyone among you not to think more highly of himself than he ought to think; but to think so as to have sound judgment, as God has allotted to each a measure of faith. (Romans 12:1-3, NASB)

A key phrase that referenced in this lecture is, "Do not be conformed to this world." The lecture introduction continues:

> In spite of their honorable intentions to engage culture for the Gospel, evangelicals often undermine the effectiveness of their own message by not understanding culture. Although evangelicals have often stood against the basic philosophical features of non-Christian world-views, at a practical level they have embraced much of what those non-Christian world-views produced by way of pop culture. This talk looks at the social habits, fads, and trends to see how, when uncritically accepted by the Church, they can be subversive to the gospel message.

A possible rationale for why this trend has occurred

within some Churches and movements is to maintain an appeal with a broader cross-section of people. It is the subtle idea attributed to H. G. Wells, "Adapt or perish, now as ever, is nature's inexorable imperative." The idea is to adapt to the changing times or lose people to the groups who do. Barbara Jordan was a Democratic Congresswoman from Texas (1972-1978). A statement attributed to her is, "We are a party of innovation. We do not reject our traditions, but we are willing to adapt to changing circumstances, when change we must. We are willing to suffer the discomfort of change in order to achieve a better future." Pope Francis is alleged to have said, "Perhaps I can say that I am a bit astute, that I can adapt to circumstances, but it is also true that I am a bit naive. Yes, but the best summary, the one that comes more from the inside and I feel most true is this: I am a sinner whom the Lord has looked upon."

All three, along with many others, suggest that circumstances are allowed to bring about adaptation and compromise in order to achieve a desired result or end. Even though a person like Barbara Jordan thoroughly knew and understood the United States Constitution, she was willing to expand her views for whatever "better good" was being proposed. A question that is seldom asked or considered by those who adapt to a particular circumstance or proposition is, "What has happened to the foundational principles and core values that are indispensable to a focused per-son and nation?

Ronald Reagan is hailed as the most recent President who was elected for and expected to maintain strong, exact conservative principles. Excerpts from *An American Life*, his autobiography, posted on August 07, 2003, included the following:

> When I began entering into the give and take of legislative bargaining in Sacramento, a lot of the most radical conservatives who had supported me during the election didn't like it. Compromise was a dirty word to

> them and they wouldn't face the fact that we couldn't get all of what we wanted today. They wanted all or nothing and they wanted it all at once. If you don't get it all, some said, don't take anything. I'd learned while negotiating union contracts that you seldom got everything you asked for. And I agreed with FDR (Franklin Delano Roosevelt), who said in 1933: I have no expectations of making a hit every time I come to bat. What I seek is the highest possible batting average. If you got seventy-five or eighty percent of what you were asking for, I say, you take it and fight for the rest later, and that's what I told these radical conservatives who never got used to it.

Should the Church be one where adapting and compromise is present in order to capture the "better good" and whatever Church growth may occur? Should God's purpose ever be relegated to man's interpretations and modified applications? Romans 12:1-3 (MSG) captures the force of what Paul wrote and God intended.

> So here's what I want you to do, God helping you: Take your everyday, ordinary life - your sleeping, eating, going-to-work, and walking-around life - and place it before God as an offering. Embracing what God does for you is the best thing you can do for him. Don't become so well-adjusted to your culture that you fit into it without even thinking. Instead, fix your attention on God. You'll be changed from the inside out. Readily recognize what he wants from you, and quickly respond to it. Unlike the culture around you, always dragging you down to its level of immaturity, God brings the best out of you, develops well-formed maturity in you. I'm speaking to you out of deep gratitude for all that God has given me, and especially as I have responsibilities in relation to you. Living then, as every one of you does, in pure grace, it's

important that you not misinterpret yourselves as people who are bringing this goodness to God. No, God brings it all to you. The only accurate way to understand ourselves is by what God is and by what he does for us, not by what we are and what we do for him.

When the Church tries to be what it isn't supposed to be, it comes across as being artificial and insincere. Additionally, the attempt to appeal to a larger cross-section of people will soon wane. A Church cannot maintain mechanically that which can only be accomplished spiritually. It seems as though the Church at large has decided to become whatever is necessary to gain new attenders and members. This is different from the Apostle Paul's commitment when he said, I Corinthians 9:19-23 (NIV).

> Though I am free and belong to no one, I have made myself a slave to everyone, to win as many as possible. To the Jews I became like a Jew, to win the Jews. To those under the law I became like one under the law (though I myself am not under the law), so as to win those under the law. To those not having the law I became like one not having the law (though I am not free from God's law but am under Christ's law), so as to win those not having the law. To the weak I became weak, to win the weak. I have become all things to all people so that by all possible means I might save some. I do all this for the sake of the gospel, that I may share in its blessings.

What did Paul mean? Did he seek to adapt and compromise? Was he neglecting any of the foundational principles and core values to which he was committed? We glean the following insights from *Matthew Henry's Concise Commentary*.

> It is the glory of a minister to deny himself, that he may serve Christ and save souls. But when a minister gives up

his right for the sake of the gospel, he does more than his charge and office demands. By preaching the gospel, freely, the apostle showed that he acted from principles of zeal and love, and thus enjoyed much comfort and hope in his soul. And though he looked on the ceremonial law as a yoke taken off by Christ, yet he submitted to it, that he might work upon the Jews, do away their prejudices, prevail with them to hear the gospel, and win them over to Christ. Though he would transgress no laws of Christ, to please any man, yet he would accommodate himself to all men, where he might do it lawfully, to gain some. Doing good was the study and business of his life; and, that he might reach this end, he did not stand on privileges. We must carefully watch against extremes, and against relying on anything but trust in Christ alone. We must not allow errors or faults, so as to hurt others, or disgrace the gospel.

In his *Exposition of the Whole Bible*, John Gill adds this commentary.

> To the weak became I as weak....That is, to weak Christians, who were weak in faith, and had not such clear knowledge of Gospel liberty, and therefore scrupled the eating of some sorts of meat, and particularly meats offered to idols; and the apostle so far consulted the peace and edification of these weak brethren, and so far complied with them, and became as one of them, that, rather than offend them, he determined to eat no meat while the world stood: that I might gain the weak; promote their edification and welfare, who otherwise might be stumbled, be in danger of falling from, and laid under a temptation to desert the faith of the gospel.

James Perry

Maintaining the status quo at any and all costs sounds appealing, but it is shortsighted. The Church that is declining in attendance and membership is a Church that has allowed the status quo to become their norm. In the process, they have forgotten to maintain a vision and sense of mission to reach the lost with the Gospel of the Lord Jesus Christ. It may be nice to have attractive and extravagant buildings in which to meet but store fronts are also an effective way to bring the Church to the people. As attractive as it was designed and built to be, the Crystal Cathedral in Garden Grove (Orange County) California, amassed significant debt (more than 50 million dollars) and was forced to file for Bankruptcy. Other Churches close quietly when they are no longer able to maintain their current expenses and ministry. The landscape of our nation is dotted with Church buildings that once house a group of people with professed faith and hope. They aged and withered. The building is now one that is a skeleton of the past and is crumbling. A sad and descriptive view of what can happen with a Church that does not maintain a viable and fruitful ministry can be gleaned by looking at deserted and abandoned buildings in Detroit (after the city defaulted on its debt), Michigan (http://www.timesunion.com/news/article/The-abandoned-buildings-of-Detroit-4674912.php#photo-4931773). A Church must either move out of its comfort zone (status quo which is unacceptable) or suffer the grim consequences as it becomes a vacated, deserted and abandoned monument of what used to be and what might've been. What should the Church and follower of Jesus Christ be? The Bible explains in Ephesians 5:13-20 (NIV).

> But everything exposed by the light becomes visible and everything that is illuminated becomes a light. This is why it is said: Wake up, sleeper, rise from the dead, and Christ will shine on you. Be very careful, then, how you live, not as unwise but as wise, making the most of every opportunity, because the days are evil. Therefore do not be foolish, but understand what the Lord's will is. Do

THE TWENTY-FIRST CENTURY CHURCH: IS IT WAXING OR WANING?

> not get drunk on wine, which leads to debauchery. Instead, be filled with the Spirit, speaking to one another with psalms, hymns, and songs from the Spirit. Sing and make music from your heart to the Lord, always giving thanks to God the Father for everything, in the name of our Lord Jesus Christ.

Matthew Henry's Concise Commentary indicates how the Christian needs to live and what the message of the Church must be in order to maximize its effectiveness.

> Walk as children of light, as having knowledge and holiness. These works of darkness are unfruitful, whatever profit they may boast; for they end in the destruction of the impenitent sinner. There are many ways of abetting, or taking part in the sins of others; by commendation, counsel, consent, or concealment. And if we share with others in their sins, we must expect to share in their plagues. If we do not reprove the sins of others, we have fellowship with them. A good man will be ashamed to speak of what many wicked men are not ashamed to do. We must have not only a sight and a knowledge that sin is sin, and in some measure shameful, but see it as a breach of God's holy law. After the example of prophets and apostles, we should call on those asleep and dead in sin, to awake and arise, that Christ may give them light.

In 1826, Bernard Barton wrote the words by which one can live. It also serves as a challenge for a Church to move beyond and away from an unacceptable status quo approach into a more Biblical role and focused ministry.

> *Walk in the light: and sin abhorred*
> *Shall never defile again;*

James Perry

The blood of Jesus Christ, thy Lord,
Shall cleanse from every stain.

Walk in the light: and thou shalt find
Thy heart made truly His
Who dwells in cloudless light enshrined
In whom no darkness is.

Walk in the light: and thine shall be
A path, though thorny, bright;
For God, by grace, shall dwell in thee,
And God Himself is light.

4. Form and Function

And they came to Capernaum. And when He was in the house he asked them, "What were you discussing on the way?" But they kept silent, for on the way they had argued with one another about who was the greatest. And he sat down and called the twelve. And he said to them, If anyone would be first, he must be last of all and servant of all. And he took a child and put him in the midst of them, and taking him in his arms, he said to them, Whoever receives one such child in my name receives me, and whoever receives me, receives not me but him who sent me.
Mark 9:33-37 (ESV)

One of the sad truths about the visible Church is the presence of a pecking order that allows for some to be deemed more important than others. A person of wealth is easily viewed as being more vital than a person of poverty. A well educated person is deemed to be one who knows more than the one who dropped out of school. When these truths exist, a community begins to form an opinion about those who are more prominent than others. As a result, a local Church, rightly or wrongly, gains a reputation and image that affects whether or not any will be interested in attending or seeking to become a member. People draw their own conclusion about the visible Church in terms of whether it represents more form than function. Viability pertains to what a visible Church is committed to doing. Any functional Church should be able to be measured by The Book of James. One of the many lessons approached by James is 2:14-19:

> What good is it, my brothers and sisters, if someone claims to have faith but has no deeds? Can such faith save them? Suppose a brother or a sister is without clothes and daily food. If one of you says to them, Go in peace; keep warm and well fed, but does nothing about

their physical needs, what good is it? In the same way, faith by itself, if it is not accompanied by action, is dead. But someone will say, You have faith; I have deeds. Show me your faith without deeds, and I will show you my faith by my deeds. You believe that there is one God. Good! Even the demons believe that—and shudder.

An attitude that speaks about a needy person and allows the erudite or superior one to state, sometimes coarsely or abruptly, "Give them $20.00 and get rid of them" is the wrong attitude. When this occurs it is a clear violation of the instruction in James 2. A visible Church is measured by whether or not it merely talks the talk or actually walks the walk. The visible Church should be committed to doing deeds of righteousness and care, rather than just speaking the words apart from any meaningful and purposeful action. There was a Church that reluctantly granted its permission to hire a youth minister who would try to reach children in the community. He was successful in this ministry and children were beginning to regularly come and participate in youth-oriented and Church activities. They came as they were and more often than not they weren't neatly dressed. One of the things gleaned from this ministry is that most of the children were coming from homes that were struggling. The children were hungry. It was decided to have a supper primarily for the children. It wasn't fancy but it was more than they were used to having at home. The supper became the center piece for the youth who were meeting and the evening service that followed. Perhaps it was an error in judgment, but the supper and evening service became attached. Remember, the supper was being provided for the children and was now being expanded so the adults could share in the overall ministry. The idea was for the adults to interact with the children and model genuine care for them. The best plan and idea cannot always achieve its goal. When some of the children entered the fellowship hall for the supper, one of the older adults growled at them for wearing their cap into the Church. When the supper was ready, the older adults were the first in line to get the food they wanted for themselves. Those who were better-off behaved as though they were more-deserving and had to be first before the children picked over the food that had been provided. The ministry to the children was flourishing but it was soon concluded by the decision-makers of the Church to terminate the youth minister. The inevitable happened. The one who had ministered so effectively with the children was no longer there and the children slowly departed and were no longer coming. One can always look back with hindsight and live in the "if only" world. In some instances, a Church has one chance to do what's right and to continue it faithfully. Once there is a breach and unnecessary change occurs, a ministry may have to endure a chain-reaction impact in an overall diminishing ministry. This Church that behaved so poorly is struggling to survive. With mostly aging members and no younger families, it is questionable how much longer it will be able to continue. It demonstrates that a legacy of a previous generation has become a negative in terms of Church survival.

    The public and community are wise in terms of what is practical and necessary. They are perceptive in terms of a Church's priorities. Even though they may base their present mindsets based upon past impressions, they do not believe they would be welcomed and accepted in a particular Church setting and organization. They also see and understand when a visible Church is more focused on costly buildings and expenditures to maintain a physical plant. It doesn't matter if the Church has a missionary budget that supports God's servants who are ministering to people groups and cultures all over the world. That which is significant to the public and person outside of the Church structure is whether or not a similar ministry in a local setting is as meaningful as the one supported thousands of miles away. A prominent Church was supporting missionaries where the people were black-skinned. The missionaries had done a magnificent and appreciated ministry among the people.

Churches had been started and people were turning to Jesus Christ and away from their traditional false religion. The President of the Council of Churches in that nation came to the United States to offer his gratitude to the Churches for sending the missionaries to them. One large congregation in the South had their leaders stand at the door of the Church and refuse this man admission. Why? The only reason was that he was black-skinned. The Churches elsewhere that did allow him entrance received considerable blessing through his manner and ministry. James 2:1-7 (NIV) warns the professing Christian and the Church:

> My brothers and sisters, believers in our glorious Lord Jesus Christ must not show favoritism. Suppose a man comes into your meeting wearing a gold ring and fine clothes, and a poor man in filthy old clothes also comes in. If you show special attention to the man wearing fine clothes and say, Here's a good seat for you, but say to the poor man, You stand there or sit on the floor by my feet, have you not discriminated among yourselves and become judges with evil thoughts? Listen, my dear brothers and sisters: Has not God chosen those who are poor in the eyes of the world to be rich in faith and to inherit the kingdom he promised those who love him? But you have dishonored the poor. Is it not the rich who are exploiting you? Are they not the ones who are dragging you into court? Are they not the ones who are blaspheming the noble name of him to whom you belong?

What is James talking about here? He is warning the believer against showing favoritism or partiality. It means the propensity (a natural inclination or tendency) of the Church to pay special attention to a person because of his wealth, social standing, position, authority, popularity, looks, appearance, skin-pigmentation or influence. The Church mentioned above came to a point where it was no longer able to continue as a viable

THE TWENTY-FIRST CENTURY CHURCH: IS IT WAXING OR WANING

Church entity. The building and facility that had denied a black-skinned servant of God admission is now inhabited by a vibrant and thriving bi-racial congregation.

When a Church becomes preoccupied with structures and their maintenance, and is showing preference and partiality toward certain people, it will negatively impact a Church in many significant ways. Obligations to the Church as a building structure becomes a major budget focus. As the reality of budgetary needs is a primary consideration, it will mean that budget adjustments may have to be made in terms of mission and ministry. Support of missionaries will be lessened. Necessary staff reductions may be required. Outreach and care for the widows, orphans and the poor will be reduced or eliminated. Monies that were pledged for building and expansion are not always given. The "form" has short-circuited the "function" of what the Church was designed to be and do for Jesus Christ. When the public forms an opinion that there is classification within a Church of the greater to the lesser and it is perceived to be the reality, those who either resent the perceived presence of such or their failure to be included among them, will lose interest and not be ready to sacrifice to make the visible Church's needs to be met. When a form (building) becomes the focal point, the function for which it was constructed becomes fuzzy and unclear. It is at this point that people become disillusioned and begin to drift away. They may even arrive at the place of being numbered with the "nones" (those who no longer identify with any particular religion and who have become the religiously unaffiliated) or "dones" (a group of once-dedicated Church members who have decided to stop going to Church; they are fatigued with the Sunday routine of plop, pray and pay). Their disillusionment has become so great that they may never again enter a structure that identifies itself as a Church of the Lord Jesus Christ. Are they correct for feeling and acting in this manner? Why do you enter the Church building where people are supposed to gather for worship of the Living God and to sense His presence in their midst? Can the Worship Service be deemed to be an "Order of Worship" or has it become in actuality a "Disorder of Worship"? Are things being done because in the Worship Service that will draw a person closer to the Lord and His will, or are the parts of the Service detached from one another with no connection to the Word of God that is proclaimed? Some people get the impression that things are included in a Service because someone might be offended if The Apostles' Creed or The Lord's Prayer was not recited. Has this become part of a ritual (form) or is it vibrant and meaningful experience (function) for those present? If a person entering or leaving the Church was asked, "What do you believe the focus and message of this Church is," would they know? What would their response be?

When I was a boy, my Mother took her three children to a Church whose focus and commitment was emblazoned clearly above the portals through which people would enter. The mission and message of the Church was plainly stated for all passersby to see. Engraved in stone were the words: "We preach Christ - Crucified, Risen and Coming Again!" If Jesus Christ was writing the inscription above the portals of many Churches today, He might etch with His finger just one word: "Ichabod" (without honor; the glory is departed from this place). What would He etch above the portals of the Church you are attending, supporting and perpetuating? If one is candid, it might cause a review to make certain that Ichabod is not God's assessment for the Church in which you are involved and engaged.

It is a sad and grievous day when the glory of the Lord is gone from a Church. It is even more acute when those who attend the Church don't see or know the difference and Church business continues as it always has and always will. The *Westminster Shorter Catechism* asks and answers, "What is the chief end of man?" "Man's chief end is to glorify God, and to enjoy him forever." Two of the Scripture texts indicated for the answer are: 1 Corinthians 6:20 and 10:31 (KJV). "For you are bought with a price: therefore glorify God in your body, and in your spirit, which are God's. Whether therefore ye eat, or drink, or whatsoever ye do, do all to the glory of God." The prominence and centrality that is to be present in one's life and actions should also be present in the Church. Historically, that has not always been the case. An example in this regard is The Book of Ezekiel, especially Chapters 9 through 11 that speak of the Glory of God departing from the Temple. The four-step sequence begins to unfold with great flurry and sound. However, no one is listening, observing or showing any concern. God's Glory begins to depart from the temple (9:3; 10:4) and the glory cloud fills the temple one last time (10:4). Once again, no one is there to notice or show any concern. The people are not seeing or hearing. The glory of God, with the cherubim, moves and stands at the East gate, the entrance of the temple (10:18-19). One would think that this would be observable and require someone pleading with the Lord for mercy and forgiveness. No one does so and no one seems to care. They are busy with the temporal things of life and the Temple and what it was supposed to represent were far-removed from their perception. After lingering for a time, the Glory Cloud then moves to the mount overlooking the city and Temple (11:23). Yet again, no one notices or pays attention. No one seemingly, in their heart of hearts, cares. And then, the Glory of God departs fully and completely. The people were temporarily left with their form but was without any useful or meaningful function.

Ephesians 3:8-12 (NKJV) has this commentary on the role of the Church in its ministry to all people. Paul wrote:

> To me, who am less than the least of all the saints, this grace was given, that I should preach among the Gentiles the unsearchable riches of Christ, and to make all see what is the fellowship of the mystery, which from the beginning of the ages has been hidden in God who created all things through Jesus Christ; to the intent that

now the manifold wisdom of God might be made known by the Church to the principalities and powers in the heavenly places, according to the eternal purpose which He accomplished in Christ Jesus our Lord, in whom we have boldness and access with confidence through faith in Him.

The role of the Biblical Church is stated to be: "the intent that now the manifold wisdom of God might be made known by the Church to the principalities and powers in the heavenly places, according to the eternal purpose which He accomplished in Christ Jesus our Lord." Paul is speaking of the spiritual warfare in which the Church of Jesus Christ is to be engaged. The Church can conduct this ministry fearlessly and forthrightly. The principality and powers cannot limit the mission or message of the Church. As an encouragement, Paul had written in Romans 8:38-39 (NKJV), " For I am persuaded that neither death nor life, nor angels nor principalities nor powers, nor things present nor things to come, nor height nor depth, nor any other created thing, shall be able to separate us from the love of God which is in Christ Jesus our Lord." When we attach these words with those in Ephesians 3:20-21 (NKJV) we should be both emboldened and encouraged because of our confidence in The One of Whom it is said, "Now to Him who is able to do exceedingly abundantly above all that we ask or think, according to the power that works in us, to Him be glory in the Church by Christ Jesus to all generations, forever and ever. Amen!" Never allow yourself to be cowered into or subverted by a false loyalty to form. Your subscription and commitment should be to the function of the Biblical Church as it does God's work in God's way.

The website, *Compelling Truth* (http://compellingtruth.org), has this entry for the purpose for which God established His Church. In part, it states:

> The Church is the body of Christ, a group of people

THE TWENTY-FIRST CENTURY CHURCH: IS IT WAXING OR WANING

unified (Ephesians 4:1-3) under Christ, who represent and reflect Him to the world (1 Corinthians 12:12-17). The purpose of the Church is to join people of different backgrounds and talents and provide them training and opportunities for God's work. It accomplishes this both internally, within the body, and externally, in the world. Acts 2:42 explains the internal function of the Church: And they devoted themselves to the apostles' teaching and the fellowship, to the breaking of bread and the prayers. Jesus entrusted the Church with the task to teach the body sound doctrine…God entrusted His word to the Church (Ephesians 4:14). Knowledge of doctrine is useless if it isn't used (1 Corinthians 13:2): So Christ himself gave the apostles, the prophets, the evangelists, the pastors and teachers, to equip his people for works of service, so that the body of Christ may be built up until we all reach unity in the faith and in the knowledge of the Son of God and become mature, attaining to the whole measure of the fullness of Christ (Ephesians 4:11-13 NIV). Sound teaching leads to spiritual maturity which leads to building up the body of Christ.

The center and foundation for all that is done is anchored to the Bible. If there is any hesitancy or marginalization when it comes to the inspiration of God's Word, it will erode and diminish the purpose God has for His people and His Church. The basic subscription to the Bible is in terms of plenary (in its' entirety), verbal (every word without exception) and inspiration (breathed out by God to make it the living Word of God for all who believe). An evangelist, before he began his sermon, would often cite the following:

How Should I Approach The Bible?
Think of it carefully. Study it prayerfully.

James Perry

Deep in your heart let its oracles dwell.
Ponder its mystery; Slight not its history;
For none ever loved it too fondly or well.

In 1917, Haldor Lillenas wrote the words to an important and meaningful hymn that should encourage God's people to be faithful and obedient to God's Word and mandates.

The Bible stands like a rock undaunted
'Mid the raging storms of time;
Its pages burn with the truth eternal,
And they glow with a light sublime.

The Bible stands like a mountain towering
Far above the works of men;
Its truth by none ever was refuted,
And destroy it they never can.

Refrain

The Bible stands though the hills may tumble,
It will firmly stand when the earth shall crumble;
I will plant my feet on its firm foundation,
For the Bible stands.

5. Highway of Holiness

Do your best to present yourself to God as one approved, a worker who has no need to be ashamed, rightly handling the word of truth. But avoid irreverent babble, for it will lead people into more and more ungodliness, and their talk will spread like gangrene...
II Timothy 2:15-17 (ESV)

What is the Church called to be, to do and to endure? The intention was never for the Church to be continually adapting itself to rituals, forms, secular influences or cultural values. The people of God have been called to a much higher value system and practice of religion. The value system is not found in the forms that are imposed, the rituals that are followed or the programs that have been developed. Before one can be what God wants him to be, it is necessary to know God's purpose for each person in relationship with Him. How did one become a child of God and what is His will and purpose for His children?

On August 11, 2011, *USA Today* reviewed a telecast of "The Colbert Report." The Headline of the report was: "Stephen Colbert questions God's job performance." In his satirical format, Colbert ranted: "We're mad at Congress, mad at President Obama, mad at Wall Street. Can't anyone live up to their job description? What about God? How's His performance these days?" While his routine bordered on being sacrilegious, we can and should give serious consideration about God and His performance as it pertains to His relationship to a people who are included in the Bride of Christ, the Church. The broader question of Colbert on God's job performance is thought provoking. If we were being asked that question directly, what would our response be? One possible suggestion would focus on, "is God being acknowledged in all of our ways?" As we think about Colbert's question regarding God's job performance, let us reflect on Who God is and some of what we know He does. One foundational answer to this broad question is that God always acts in accordance with His character, purpose, nature, will and attributes. The *Westminster Shorter Catechism* asks: "What is God?" The response given is: "God is a Spirit (John 4:24), infinite (Psalm 147:3, 5), eternal (Psalm 90:2), and unchangeable (Hebrews 1:12), in his being (I Timothy 6:15-16), wisdom (Psalm 104:24), power (Matthew 19:26), holiness (I Peter 1:15-16), justice (Exodus 34:6-7), goodness (Psalm 103:5), and truth (Psalm 86:15). We know that He cannot and does not lie (Hebrews 6:18 and Titus 1:2); God cannot and will not deny Himself (II Timothy 2:11-13) and He is unlimited in terms of what He can and will do (Psalm 147:5 and Ephesians 3:20)." Our foundational answer should be Ephesians 1:3-11 (ESV). This passage gives an initial response regarding the performance of God. His performance is not a theatrical act but an eternal plan that He set in motion before the world began (I Peter 1:18-20). Ephesians 1 is not an exhaustive list but a starting place of what God has done according to the purpose of His eternal plan and will. It would be appropriate to think of this passage as being God's reclamation plan. The text begins, "Blessed be the God and Father of our Lord Jesus Christ." That statement is then amplified with eleven things God has done to bring a people unto Himself, a people who will comprise the Bride of Christ: He has blessed us in Christ with every spiritual blessing in the heavenly places; He chose us in him before the foundation of the world, that we should be holy and blameless before him; In love He predestined us; He adopted us as sons and daughters through Jesus Christ; Our adoption was according to the purpose of his will, to the praise of his glorious grace, with which he has blessed us in the Beloved; (Through The Beloved) We have redemption through His blood; We have the forgiveness of our sins and trespasses; He lavished His grace upon us, in all wisdom and insight; We are the benefactors of the riches of His grace that He has made known to us the mystery of his will, according to his purpose, which he set forth in Christ as a plan for the fullness of time, to unite all things in him, things in heaven and things on earth; We have obtained an inheritance in Christ, having been predestined according to the purpose of him who works all things according to the counsel of his will.

The words of the third stanza written by P.P. Bliss (1875) summarize one's condition prior to the forgiveness that was granted to one in Jesus Christ:

> *Guilty, vile, and helpless we;*
> *Spotless Lamb of God was He;*
> *"Full atonement!" can it be?*
> *Hallelujah!*
> *What a Savior!*

In like manner, the fourth stanza of And Can It Be? - Charles Wesley (1738) amplifies this conclusion:

> *Long my imprisoned spirit lay,*
> *Fast bound in sin and nature's night;*
> *My chains fell off, my heart was free,*
> *I rose, went forth, and followed Thee.*

The second point indicated above states: He chose us in him before the foundation of the world, that we should be holy and blameless before him is stated in the NLT: "Long ago, even before he made the world, God loved us and chose us in Christ to be holy and without fault in his eyes." His unchanging plan has always been to adopt us into his own family by bringing us to himself through Jesus Christ. Holiness is stated as an achievable goal for every child of God who is in Jesus Christ. Hebrews 12:14-15 (NIV), "Make every effort to live in peace with everyone and to be holy; without holiness no one will see the Lord. See to it that no one falls short of the grace of God and that no bitter root grows up to cause trouble and defile many." As one proceeds on the journey of faith and hope, and as the destination of that journey becomes more clear in our focus, the reality and benefit of having walked in God's ways and will are expressed in Isaiah 35:8-10 (NIV).

> And a highway will be there; it will be called the Way of Holiness; it will be for those who walk on that Way. The unclean will not journey on it; wicked fools will not go about on it. No lion will be there, nor any ravenous beast; they will not be found there. But only the redeemed will walk there, and those the Lord has rescued will return. They will enter Zion with singing; everlasting joy will crown their heads. Gladness and joy will overtake them, and sorrow and sighing will flee away.

The "Way of Holiness" commands our attention. What is implied and stated on God's Highway of Holiness? What is required of the one who desires to walk on and in the "Way of Holiness"? The basic and minimum requirement is given to us in I Peter 1:13-16 (NASB). Peter writes a formulation toward holiness when he writes to the believers.

> Therefore, prepare your minds for action, keep sober in spirit, fix your hope completely on the grace to be brought to you at the revelation of Jesus Christ. As obedient children, do not be conformed to the former lusts which were yours in your ignorance, but like the Holy One who called you, be holy yourselves also in all your behavior; because it is written: You shall be holy, for I am holy.

Peter is quoting and reinforcing the stated will of God from Leviticus 11:44 and 19:2. All of what God is and does is based upon His holiness. It is foundational to Who God is and is the underpinning of His attributes. When one speaks of God is love, it is a holy love. The mercy of God, it is a holy mercy. The

THE TWENTY-FIRST CENTURY CHURCH: IS IT WAXING OR WANING

Law given to Moses was a holy law that revealed His character. The Law serves to demonstrate what a person is to believe about God and to learn His requirements for one's interactional behavior. It should be understood that even His judgments, wrath and anger are holy. In all of who and what God is, He is perfectly and absolutely holy.

The emphasis of Scripture that Peter is repeating (I Peter 1:16) represents his addressing the true believers in the Lord Jesus Christ. They are facing imminent persecution during the reign of Nero. Peter is reiterating that the culture and world should not be allowed to dictate a believer's worldview or behavior. To be sanctified or holy has a singular application. It means that one is to be set apart to the Lord and to be distancing oneself from the world and its influences. The true believer is to be living by God's standards, not the world's. While perfection is the ultimate goal and necessity for entrance into God's heaven, God's calling us is not to be totally perfect now but to be distinct from the world. We should remember and be thankful for God's provision for us in Jesus Christ. II Corinthians 5:21 states: "He made Him who knew no sin to be sin on our behalf, so that we might become the righteousness of God in Him." Our perfection and holiness is in Christ and not in our works or any pietistic exercises one contrives. If one is separated from the world and its influences, then I Peter 2:9 identifies that one as being a citizen of a holy nation. Note the verse and how Peter describes the true believer, "But you are a chosen people, a royal priesthood, a holy nation, a people belonging to God, that you may declare the praises of him who called you out of darkness into his wonderful light" (NIV). Peter is establishing that the believers are to be separated from the world. It also is indicating that one needs to live out that reality in day-to-day living and lifestyle choices. Such a one is also to be a beacon of light that penetrates into and through the darkness of the culture and world.

James Perry

The only way one can become holy is the result of a right relationship with God through Jesus Christ. There are different expressions one can use such as, being saved or accepting Jesus Christ as Savior. The true believer understands that positionally he is now in Jesus Christ and has begun his journey on the highway of holiness as he abides in Christ. In Christ, one has been set apart from the world. Because of this position that is now ours in Christ, we are to live a distinct, set-apart life from the world. The notion that one must find acceptance in the world is bogus. It is a view totally rejected by Jesus Christ and the Word of God. The idea that one needs to blend into the world around him and to find acceptance within the culture is detrimental to what a set-apart believer is to be and become. With this new relationship in Christ, there is also a new commitment one makes. The minimum response one should make to God's purpose for us in Christ should be a prayer flowing from the depths of our being. It should be a prayer of sincerity and commitment. Words of devotion and commitment that could contribute positively to one's prayer are expressed in the hymn attributed to Dallan Forgaill, translated from ancient Irish to English by Mary E. Byrne (1905). The music is from Irish folk origin.

Be Thou my Vision, O Lord of my heart;
Naught be all else to me, save that Thou art.
Thou my best Thought, by day or by night,
Waking or sleeping, Thy presence my light.

Be Thou my Wisdom, and Thou my true Word;
I ever with Thee and Thou with me, Lord;
Thou my great Father, I Thy true son;
Thou in me dwelling, and I with Thee one.

High King of Heaven, my victory won,
May I reach Heaven's joys, O bright Heaven's Sun!
Heart of my own heart, whatever befall,
Still be my Vision, O Ruler of all.

THE TWENTY-FIRST CENTURY CHURCH: IS IT WAXING OR WANING

Reflecting back on statements from Ephesians 1:3-11, we note: "He lavished His grace upon us, in all wisdom and insight" and "we are the benefactors of the riches of his grace" (Verses 7-8). As we travel the Highway of Holiness, one should always be mindful of the love, mercy and grace of God. This is the wonderful grace of Jesus that called one to be at peace with God. Think upon the preponderance of the riches of His grace which He made to abound toward us in His Son, Jesus Christ. When the Reformers began to emphasize the reality of the grace of God to-ward sinners and the practical application of that grace to individual lives, they summed up the necessity for the Christian faith and hope in a formulation that is called the Five Solas. They come from five Latin phrases (or slogans) that emerged as a result of the Protestant Reformation. The intention was that this would summarize the Reformer's basic theological beliefs. "Sola" is Latin meaning "alone" or "only" and the corresponding phrases are: Sola Fide, by faith alone; Sola Scriptura, by Scripture alone; Solus Christus, through Christ alone; Sola Gratia, by grace alone; and Soli Deo Gloria, for the glory to God alone.

In a statement about grace alone, The Cambridge Declaration of the Alliance of Confessing Evangelicals (1996) stated:

> In salvation we are rescued from God's wrath by his grace alone. It is the supernatural work of the Holy Spirit that brings us to Christ by releasing us from our bondage to sin and raising us from spiritual death to spiritual life. It is denied that salvation is in any sense a human work. Human methods, techniques or strategies by themselves cannot accomplish this transformation.

It is by this grace alone that one finds his place on the highway of holiness. When we remember what we once were outside of Christ and now traveling on the highway of holiness, we can appreciate more fully what we have been privileged to become by God's grace alone. Paul emphasizes this in Ephesians 2:1-5 (NASB):

> And you were dead in your trespasses and sins, in which you formerly walked according to the course of this world, according to the prince of the power of the air, of the spirit that is now working in the sons of disobedience. Among them we too all formerly lived in the lusts of our flesh, indulging the desires of the flesh and of the mind, and were by nature children of wrath, even as the rest.

We were living an existence devoid of hope and peace. However, the Sovereign God acted in human history to make it possible for a pathway of escape from the quagmire of sin, darkness and the enslavement within the cultural maze. There is neither print large enough nor voice loud enough to proclaim what God has done for us. Paul continues in Ephesians 2 with these resounding words, "But God, being rich in mercy, because of His great love with which He loved us, even when we were dead in our transgressions, made us alive together with Christ by grace you have been saved."

Throughout the years and generations, hymn writers have attempted to capture the significance of the grace of God acting in human history to bring about redemption and forgiveness through His Son, our Savior, Jesus Christ. Hymns such as "Amazing Grace," "Marvelous Grace of Our Loving Lord," and "Wonderful Grace of Jesus" are just a sampling of words and music expressing the great love of a Great God. A more recent hymn expresses what God has done for us "In Christ Alone." One of the stanzas contains these words, "What heights of love, what depths of peace…Here in the love of Christ I stand."

As you travel along the Highway of Holiness, there is additional benefit to the grace of God in the practical areas of one's life. There is His faithful provision for His people, II Corinthians 9:8 (NASB), "And God is able to make all grace abound to you, so that having all sufficiency in all things at all times, you may abound in every good work." Who can begin to measure the dimension of God's abounding grace? Additionally, as one experiences physical needs and challenges, God is always faithful and caring. In II Corinthians 12:9-10 (NASB), Paul wrote about his own personal experiences and the provision of God's grace in and for all of them. He wrote:

> But he said to me, My grace is sufficient for you, for my power is made perfect in weakness. Therefore I will boast all the more gladly of my weaknesses, so that the power of Christ may rest upon me. For the sake of Christ, then, I am content with weaknesses, insults, hardships, persecutions, and calamities. For when I am weak, then I am strong.

Paul was reminded of the all-sufficient grace for every need or trial he might encounter. This same all-sufficient grace is available for each of us who believe and faithfully follow the Lord Jesus Christ.

There is an interesting principle stated about God's faithful provision in Proverbs 11:24-25. The text expresses the place for one's willingness to demonstrate care and to share with others. "One gives freely, yet grows all the richer; another withholds what he should give, and only suffers want. Whoever brings blessing will be enriched, and one who waters will himself be watered" (NASB). It speaks to us of the Lord's purpose and provision for others and how he uses people to minister to other people in tangible ways. It is all occurring and is couched in the words, by His grace alone. The ministry privilege includes the words shared in Isaiah 40:1, "Comfort, comfort my people, says your God." Each of us has the capacity to interact with others who so desperately need to experience the gentleness, love, care and comfort that one should be ready to impart. The manner by which this interaction should occur is by the example shared in Isaiah 40:10-11, "Behold, the Lord God comes with might, and his arm rules for him; behold, his reward is with him, and his recompense before him. He will tend his flock like a shepherd; he will gather the lambs in his arms; he will carry them in his bosom, and gently lead those that are with young." This is the example and model we are to emulate. We are to have and show a similar care and compassion for God's sheep and His little lambs. Traveling on the Highway of Holiness never negates the place for being encouraged by and communicating to others the reality of the presence of the Lord with His sheep and lambs. Isaiah 41:10 and 13 is the message of hope and encouragement we are to embrace and communicate:

> Fear not, for I am with you; be not dismayed, for I am your God; I will strengthen you, I will help you, I will uphold you with my righteous right hand. For I, the Lord your God, hold your right hand; it is I who say to you, Fear not, I am the one who helps you.

As you walk along the Highway of Holiness, are you purposing to stand perfect and complete in all the will of God by the grace of God alone?

As we journey on the Highway of Holiness, we need to remember that Holiness is within our grasp when we have completely yielded ourselves to Jesus Christ. It is then and only then, that we enter into all of what Jesus Christ is made to be for us who believe. Read I Corinthians 1:26-31 and glean these words: "…But by His doing you are in Christ Jesus, who became to us wisdom from God, and righteousness and sanctification, and redemption…" Ponder these words and be thankful to the Lord that what we are expected to be is made possible for all who are in Jesus Christ. If that is where you are positionally, there is no valid excuse for one to be any less than what God requires us to be. We should couple with this II Corinthians

THE TWENTY-FIRST CENTURY CHURCH: IS IT WAXING OR WANING

5:21: "He made Him who knew no sin to be sin on our behalf, so that we might become the righteousness of God in Him." In 1906, Charles P. Jones wrote a hymn, "All I Need." Some of the lyric is…

Jesus Christ is made to me, All I need, all I need,
He alone is all my plea, He is all I need.

Refrain

Wisdom righteousness and pow'r, Holiness forevermore,
My redemption full and sure, He is all I need.

6. Highway of Perfection

Therefore you are to be perfect, as your heavenly Father is perfect.
Matthew 5:48

Therefore, since we have these promises, dear friends, let us purify ourselves from everything that contaminates body and spirit, perfecting holiness out of reverence for God.
II Corinthians 7:1

As we have noted the significance of the Highway of Holiness, we consider the command of Jesus to His disciples in Matthew 5:48, "You are to be perfect." What does Jesus have in mind for His followers? The *Jamieson, Fauset, Brown Bible Commentary* shares these thoughts:

> "Be ye therefore, rather, "Ye shall therefore be," or "Ye are therefore to be," as My disciples and in My kingdom, that is, to be perfect or complete. Manifestly, our Lord here speaks, not of degrees of excellence, but of the kind of excellence which was to distinguish His disciples and characterize His kingdom. When therefore He adds, even as your Father which is in heaven is perfect—He refers to that full-orbed glorious completeness which is in the great Divine Model, "their Father which is in heaven."

The commentary phrase for special note is: "The kind of excellence which was to distinguish His disciples and characterize His kingdom." To journey on the Highway of Holiness, as well as the Highway of Perfection, requires care and discipline as one learns to be all of what God wants His followers to be. While the words of Jesus are stated in the absolute and are to be heeded in that way, the attainment of perfection is a process, a goal toward which one progresses day by day. In *Matthew Poole's Commentary*, there are these helpful words:

> Perfect here is not taken in that sense as it is taken in other texts of Scripture, where it signifies sincerity and uprightness, as Job 2:3, or where it signifies a comparative perfection, as Paul saith he spake to those that were perfect; but for an absolute perfection, such as is in our Father which is in heaven, and so much is signified by the proposing of our heavenly Father as our example. Nor will it therefore follow, either that this is a mere counsel, not a precept, or that an absolute perfection in holiness is a thing in this life attainable. But that it is our duty to labour for it, forgetting what is behind, and reaching forth unto those things which are before, pressing towards the mark for the prize of the high calling of God in Christ Jesus, as the apostle speaks, Philippians 3:13,14. Proverbs *perfecto est qui perfecto proximus*. God accounts him perfect who is nearest to perfection.

These comments stress the need for progress toward the goal of perfection. Paul expands on this doctrine in Philippians 3:12-17 (ESV).

> Not that I have already obtained this or am already perfect, but I press on to make it my own, because Christ Jesus has made me his own. Brothers, I do not consider that I have made it my own. But one thing I do: forgetting what lies behind and straining forward to what lies ahead, I press on toward the goal for the prize of the upward call of God in Christ Jesus. Let those of us who are mature think this way, and if in anything you think otherwise, God will reveal that also to you. Only let us

hold true to what we have attained. Brothers, join in imitating me, and keep your eyes on those who walk according to the example you have in us.

Paul introduces another area for development as one each one of us journeys of on the Highway of Holiness and the Highway of Perfection. It is his use of the phrase, "Let those of us who are mature think this way…" This broadens out one's understanding of holiness and perfection into the meaning and value of spiritual maturity. It is difficult to attempt to make too great of a distinction between holiness, perfection, sanctification and spiritual maturity. An example of this is in the basic understanding of spiritual maturity. It is a new set of priorities entering into a per-son's life and practice. It is a transforming work of God's grace where one is no longer desiring or living in accord with desires of the flesh but a reordering of one's goals and purposes as he endeavors to please God first and foremost. If spiritual maturity is to take place, it will require personal discipline, a commitment to consistency in one's life and perseverance as we seek ways to come closer to God and His ways for us. It includes doing things God wants done by us that will glorify Him and His name. We must never forget that our chief end is to glorify God and to enjoy Him forever. We will need to begin to understand more of the mind of God for His followers so we will know what will please and honor Him.

The words of II Corinthians 6:15 through 7:1 (NASB) proposes the things we are to work through and to make the appropriate changes consistent with the one who has been surrendered to God to seek and do His will. Note carefully the words of the text:

> Do not be bound together with unbelievers; for what partnership have righteousness and lawlessness, or what fellowship has light with darkness? Or what harmony has Christ with Belial, or what has a believer in common

with an unbeliever? Or what agreement has the temple of God with idols? For we are the temple of the living God; just as God said, I will dwell in them and walk among them; and I will be their God, and they shall be My people. Therefore, come out from their midst and be separate, says the Lord. And do not touch what is unclean; and I will welcome you. And I will be a father to you, and you shall be sons and daughters to Me, says the Lord Almighty. Therefore, having these promises, beloved, let us cleanse ourselves from all defilement of flesh and spirit, perfecting holiness in the fear of God.

The questions are straight-forward and require one's straight-forward response in positive behavioral response. If followed exactly as they should be, one will be taking great strides and making considerable progress as one consistently is, "cleansing oneself from all defilement of flesh and spirit, and perfecting holiness in the fear of God." To enhance our understanding, the NLT rendering of II Corinthians 7:1 is, "Let us work toward complete holiness because we fear God." These considerations and practices are often referred to as spiritual disciplines. They expand upon the commentary in paragraph one that the perfection Jesus Christ is seeking is "...the kind of excellence which was to distinguish His disciples and characterize His kingdom."

Among the life-choices required in II Corinthians 6:14 through 7:1, "Perfecting holiness in the fear of God" also includes disciplined effort to do regular Bible reading, study, prayer, fellowship, service, and stewardship. The only way one can hope to achieve these standards and goals is by the enablement of the Holy Spirit in one's life. Paul wrote in Galatians 5:16 that the clear instruction for all followers of Jesus Christ is to "walk by the Spirit" and that will keep us from being sidetracked by the attractions of things designed to appeal to the fleshly appetites of mankind. The idea in the language used and translated is to the end that one walk by the enablement of the

THE TWENTY-FIRST CENTURY CHURCH: IS IT WAXING OR WANING

Spirit. Journeying on the Highway of Holiness and the Highway of Perfection implies one is to be in motion. The journey is long and the Holy Spirit will enable us to continue on the journey. This journey is one of purpose, value and meaning. Step by step, the Spirit will be with us to strengthen, help and encourage. The refrain to an old Hymn (Author Unknown) is: "Each step I take I know that He will guide me; To higher ground He ever leads me on. Until one day the last step will be taken. Each step I take just leads me closer home." An evidence that one has come under the control and guidance of the Holy Spirit is measurable by the fruit that is evidenced in one's life. The rule of thumb is obvious. The greater the control of the Spirit the greater abundance of spiritual fruit will be evidenced. This is the primary characteristic of spiritual maturity.

In other writings (*Taking A Serious God Seriously*), II Peter 1:3-11 (NKJV) has been dealt with at length and in detail. It is included here to demonstrate that one has every possibility for the spiritual maturity required because God has made adequate provision for His followers to receive it. As you read and reread this passage, use it as a prayer supplement for each area discussed so that you may become the full measure of that which God has provided for you in Christ.

> Grace and peace be multiplied to you in the knowledge of God and of Jesus our Lord, as His divine power has given to us all things that pertain to life and godliness, through the knowledge of Him who called us by glory and virtue, by which have been given to us exceedingly great and precious promises, that through these you may be partakers of the divine nature, having escaped the corruption that is in the world through lust. But also for this very reason, giving all diligence, add to your faith virtue, to virtue knowledge, to knowledge self-control, to self-control perseverance, to perseverance godliness, to godliness brotherly kindness, and to brotherly kindness

> love. For if these things are yours and abound, you will be neither barren nor unfruitful in the knowledge of our Lord Jesus Christ. For he who lacks these things is shortsighted, even to blindness, and has forgotten that he was cleansed from his old sins. Therefore, brethren, be even more diligent to make your call and election sure, for if you do these things you will never stumble; for so an entrance will be supplied to you abundantly into the everlasting kingdom of our Lord and Savior Jesus Christ.

God alone is our source and resource. If one is to know growth in Christ and to receive strength for the journey, there has to be the realization and acceptance that all of this is a provision of the perfect love, perfect mercy and perfect grace of the perfect God who has called us to be His very own.

When the journey on the Highway of Perfection has begun, we should know that it will be an arduous one. It will require fortitude, determination, perseverance and endurance if we are to stay the course and complete the journey properly. A lesson that had been learned by Paul and shared with fellow-believers is I Corinthians 9:24-27 (NASB).

> Do you not know that those who run in a race all run, but only one receives the prize? Run in such a way that you may win. Everyone who competes in the games exercises self-control in all things. They then do it to receive a perishable wreath, but we are imperishable. Therefore I run in such a way, as not without aim; I box in such a way, as not beating the air; but I discipline my body and make it my slave, so that, after I have preached to others, I myself will not be disqualified.

When our son was in high school in Colorado, he had become a member of the Swim Team. Regardless of the best effort by the swimmer, if he did not follow the rules, there was a person observing and assessing whether or not the swimmer had competed appropriately or if he would be disqualified. I can remember the pain I felt when our son just missed touching the wall when he was in his turn to finish his lap. The judge blew her whistle and said loudly, "DQ." He finished his lap but his best effort missed by inches. Because of that slight miss of the wall, his competing effort was disqualified. We can glean the sense of what Paul meant when he wrote, in I Corinthians 9:27 (NIV), "… so that after I have preached to others, I myself will not be dis-qualified for the prize." Small things can interfere with the priorities for life and one's journey on the Highway of Perfection. Paul's concern was to maintain all the requirements of one who is qualified to finish his course or race.

Paul had something similar in his mind when he wrote about field and track events. He knew how easily one could miss the mark, be within inches or seconds, and be disqualified for that event. When he wrote to the Philippian believers, he reminded them of the place for preparation and personal discipline when entering and competing in a race. In Philippians 3:12-17, we noted previously the attitude and motivation that will determine whether or not one will compete and finish well. One of the phrases is: "But one thing I do: forgetting what lies behind and straining forward to what lies ahead, I press on toward the goal for the prize of the upward call of God in Christ Jesus." To achieve the goal and the prize, one must not allow for diversions or detours in one's life. The focus, motivation and goal should always be the purpose of one's life. In a clear and precise manner, we read in Hebrews 12:1-2, "Let us also lay aside every encumbrance and the sin which so easily entangles us, and let us run with endurance the race that is set before us, fixing our eyes on Jesus…" That which will hinder one on the Highway of Perfection (Holiness and Spiritual Maturity) are the "every encumbrance" and the "entangling sin" that become an obstacle and cause for hindrance and stumbling.

Any person who has served in the military and been engaged in combat with an enemy knew instinctively that they could not take their footlocker of possessions into the place of conflict. If they had done so, it would hinder their ability to advance quickly. It would be detrimental to the required maneuverability in the field of conflict. It would've been an encumbrance (a thing that impedes or is burdensome; a hindrance). The danger would be in the added exposure to the enemy and the divided focus of the soldier. The full focus should be on the objective and not on the stuff one drags along with him. The "stuff" will impede one and allow for vulnerability during a battle. During the years 1721-1724, Isaac Watts was preaching from I Corinthians 16:13, "Be on the alert, stand firm in the faith, act like men, be strong." On that occasion, he penned the words to the hymn, "Am I A Soldier of the Cross?" Some of the stanzas are:

Am I a soldier of the cross, A follower of the Lamb,
And shall I fear to own His cause, Or blush to speak His Name?

Must I be carried to the skies On flowery beds of ease,
While others fought to win the prize, And sailed through bloody seas?

How do you respond to the questions asked in the hymn? Are you a soldier of the cross? Are you a follower of The Lamb? Are you ashamed to be identified with Jesus Christ and His cause? Do you think you have earned a special right and privilege others don't have so that you should be permitted to relax and enjoy the flowery bed of ease? Have you rationalized that you have no foes to face for Jesus Christ? Do you believe you are entitled to a conflict exemption because you lack sufficient courage for any intense conflict? Do you claim to have identity with Post-Traumatic Stress Disorder (PTSD) prior to your engagement in any spiritual conflict in the name of Jesus Christ?

THE TWENTY-FIRST CENTURY CHURCH: IS IT WAXING OR WANING

Despite all of the biblical instruction regarding fear and anxiety, a considerable number of people struggle with the fear of the unknown and possible unintended consequences. Many times, the fear of man and situations blurs one's fear of God. It is a form of spiritual post-traumatic stress syndrome (PTSD) that is more imagined than actual. For those who actually struggle with PTSD due to military involvement and engagement, the simple diagnosis for a very complex condition is: "You feel on edge. Nightmares keep coming back. Sudden noises make you jump. You're staying at home more and more. Could you have PTSD? If you have experienced severe trauma or a life-threatening event, you may develop symptoms of post-traumatic stress, commonly known as post-traumatic stress disorder, PTSD, shell shock, or combat stress. Maybe you felt like your life or the lives of others were in danger, or that you had no control over what was happening. You may have witnessed people being injured or dying, or you may have been physically harmed yourself. There is a considerable difference and distinction between the physical PTSD and a spiritual form of it. One is actual and the other is imagined. There is counseling, treatment and medication for the actual. For the imagined, the only legitimate treatment is prayer and perseverance.

The Book of Psalms deals with a wide range of emotions and circumstances. Amid all of the spiritual struggles, prayer and perseverance always brings the person back to focus on the Lord Who is the Shepherd and the one Who cares for His sheep. In Psalm 37:1-10, David reminded himself of how one should deal with apprehensions about the unknown. Some of the words and phrases he employs are: "Do not fret…Be not envious…Trust in the Lord…Cultivate faithfulness…Delight yourself in the Lord…Commit your way to the Lord…Trust also in Him…Rest in the Lord…Wait patiently for Him…Cease from anger…Forsake wrath…the humble will inherit the land…they will delight themselves in abundant prosperity." If you expect to travel the Highway of Perfection (holiness and spiritual maturity), these personal attributes must be pre-sent and actual in how you view life and the spiritual conflict in which you are needed and expected to be engaged. Gloria Gaither wrote the words to a newer hymn, "I Then Shall Live." Some of the lyrics that touch on the journey along the Highway of Perfection (holiness and spiritual maturity) are: "I know how fear builds walls instead of bridges…" These are the barriers or barricades that prevent one's advance in both personal growth in the Lord, as well as the extent of one's engagement in the spiritual conflict. In another stanza, the words are: "Your Hallowed Name, O may I bear with honor, And may Your living Kingdom come in me." This underscores the need and place for the invisible Church being visible through us.

The invisible Church fails to be visible when those professing to be the Bride of Christ are building walls instead of bridges. Scores of individuals, parishioners and pastors alike, have left the Church because of the barriers that have been built. They have found the enemy within the Church to be formidable, almost as much as the enemy without the structure of the visible Church. Marginal attention is given to the state of the Church today. The most recent statistics (2014) complied by *The Fuller Institute; George Barna and Pastoral Care, Inc.* indicate the following reality:

> The profession of pastor is near the bottom of a survey of the most-respected professions, just above car salesman. 4,000 new Churches begin each year and 7,000 Churches close. Over 1,700 pastors left the ministry every month last year. Over 1,300 pastors were terminated by the local Church each month, many without cause. Over 3,500 people a day left the Church last year. Many denominations report an empty pulpit crisis. They cannot find ministers willing to fill positions. The number one reason pastors leave the ministry - Church people are not willing to go in the same direction and goal of the pastor. Pastors believe God wants them

to go in one direction but the people are not willing to follow or change.

Some of the power-managers within the visible Church may dispute the statistics but they cannot deny them with any validity or credibility. They need to ponder carefully and prayerfully the data that indicates: "Half of all Churches last year did not add one new member through conversion growth. Churches lose an estimated 2,765,000 people each year to nominalism and secularism." That which is sadder than the above statistics is how often the pastor becomes the subject of blame for the lack of growth and the departure of people from the Pastoral care of a particular visible Church.

The previous chapter on the Highway of Holiness concluded with words that are similarly applicable for this Chapter. An obvious truth is that no one can drift into holiness or perfection. One can only access that which God requires from one source - Jesus Christ. When we are in Him, then the words that apply for those on the Highway of Holiness are the same for this on the Highway of Perfection. Read I Corinthians 1:26-31 and take notice of these words: "…But by His doing you are in Christ Jesus, who became to us wisdom from God, and righteousness and sanctification, and redemption…" Ponder these words and be thankful to the Lord that what we are expected to be is made possible for all who are in Jesus Christ. If that is where you are positionally, there is no valid excuse for you to be any less than what God requires you to be in Christ alone. We should couple with this II Corinthians 5:21, "He made Him who knew no sin to be sin on our behalf, so that we might become the righteousness of God in Him." When Paul wrote to the Colossian Church about the necessity for Jesus Christ to be preeminent in all things, he was saying that this included our lives and our relationship to Him. He states in Colossians 1:28-29, "We proclaim Him, admonishing every man and teaching every man with all wisdom, so that we may present every man complete in Christ." To be "complete in Christ" means we have progressed in becoming holy and perfect in Him. Other translations insert the idea of our having also become spiritually mature in Jesus Christ. These verses are paraphrased in the NLT in this manner, "So we tell others about Christ, warning everyone and teaching everyone with all the wisdom God has given us. We want to present them to God, perfect in their relationship to Christ. That's why I work and struggle so hard, depending on Christ's mighty power that works within me." So there would be no doubt in anyone's mind about the source of perfection, in Colossians 1:15-20 (ESV, Selected)) Paul emphasized the following about Jesus Christ.

> He is the image of the invisible God...by him all things were created, in heaven and on earth, visible and invisible...all things were created through him and for him. And he is before all things, and in him all things hold together. And he is the head of the body, the Church...For in him all the fullness of God was pleased to dwell, and through him to reconcile to himself all things, whether on earth or in heaven, making peace by the blood of his cross.

It is in Jesus Christ alone that we possess holiness, perfection and spiritual maturity. It is in this perfect relationship that the invisible Church becomes visible within a culture that wanders in the fog of self-aggrandizement and self-centeredness. Are you walking on the Highway of Holiness, the Highway of Perfection and experiencing the fullness of spiritual maturity in Jesus Christ?

Search me, God, and know my heart;
test me and know my anxious thoughts.
See if there is any offensive way in me,
and lead me in the way everlasting.
Psalm 139:23-24 (NIV)

7. Highway of Carnality

Brothers and sisters, I could not address you as people who live by the Spirit but as people who are still worldly—mere infants in Christ. I gave you milk, not solid food, for you were not yet ready for it. Indeed, you are still not ready. You are still worldly. For since there is jealousy and quarreling among you, are you not worldly? Are you not acting like mere humans?
I Corinthians 3:1-3 (NIV)

In previous Chapters 5 and 6, we discussed the requirement of God for His people to be on the Highway of Holiness and the Highway of Perfection. These two considerations are similar and interchangeable with each other. When one is in Jesus Christ, he is in the one who is holy and perfect. Biblical History indicates that from the Garden of Eden forward different ones have made the choice to follow their carnal desires rather than going forward into spiritual maturity. When doing so, they have prevented progress in seeking after both holiness and perfection. Paul defines what he means by carnal in the text above from I Corinthians 3, "I could not address you as people who live by the Spirit, but as people who are still worldly…" They should've learned and known that trying to straddle this fence with one foot in the spiritual and the other in the world is untenable and impossible. It could be likened to a picket fence that would illustrate that it could be harmful and injurious. Why did Paul address the Corinthians as worldly and carnal?

> *Barnes Notes Of The Bible*, I Corinthians 3:1-3:
> For ye are yet carnal - Though you are Christians, and are the friends of God in the main, yet your divisions and strifes show that you are yet, in some degree, under the influence of the principles which govern the people

of this world. People who are governed solely by the principles of this world, evince a spirit of strife, emulation and contention; and just so far as you are engaged in strife, just so far do you show that you are governed by their principles and feelings.

Matthew Poole's Commentary on this text: For ye are yet carnal; not wholly carnal, but in a great measure so, not having your lusts and corrupt affections entirely subdued to the will of God, nor yet so much subdued as some other Christians have, and you ought to have. As an evidence of this he reminds them of the envying, strifes, and divisions that were among them. Strife and envying are reckoned among the works of the flesh, Galatians 5:19-21; they are all opposite to love, in which the perfection of a Christian lies.

Vincent's Word Studies on this text: Here the milder word carnal is used, having the nature of flesh. Paul would say that he was compelled to address the Corinthians as unspiritual, made of flesh. Here he says that though they have received the Spirit in some measure, they are yet under the influence of the flesh." They are a people who are unwilling or incapable of severing the appeal of worldly things from their felt need to gain spiritual maturity in Christ. The issue Paul raises is that the visible Church is to be a true and accurate reflection and demonstration of the invisible Church.

The invisible Church is marked by its certainty because it is the Bride of Christ. It is established upon eternal verities that are always certain and clearly revealed. The visible Church is to be a representation upon the earth of the invisible Church. There are distinctive marks by which the visible Church can be measured. They are: The Word of God (Holy Scripture) is central and faithfully proclaimed (free of any compromise); The

THE TWENTY-FIRST CENTURY CHURCH:
IS IT WAXING OR WANING

sacraments (Baptism and The Lord's Supper) are uncompromisingly administered; Prayer is vital communication and fellowship with the triune God; and Church discipline is consistently administered where an attender or member has committed an offense against God, The Word, the visible Church or some other entity. Another chapter has dealt with those who are classified as the "Nones" and those who are the "Dones", who no longer believe the visible Church is serving any meaningful purpose. One of the key factors with the decline within the visible Church is that too many of them are being run man's way rather than God's way. This is what was taking place in the Church at Corinth.

The above text from I Corinthians 3:1-3 is a major factor. When the visible Church is being operated in a secular way rather than in a spiritual manner, decline in attendance will be inevitable. Carnality, if allowed to go unchecked, can decimate the visible Church. There was an illustration of this fact given in chapter 6. The chapter concluded with statistics regarding the Churches and pastors. Even though some within the visible Church will dispute the statistics, there is no way that they can deny them factually. The culture has impacted the Church and it is evidenced by the carnality that prevails among Church members, as well as Church leaders. This is the force of what Paul is writing and indicating about the Corinthians who were professing believers. The compounded tension is amplified by I Corinthians 2:14 (NIV), "The person without the Spirit does not accept the things that come from the Spirit of God but considers them foolishness, and cannot understand them because they are discerned only through the Spirit." The carnal person is man-centered and allows no room for spiritual truths to permeate his life. Such a person views himself as self-made and not making time or room for any divine interaction.

The tension between the spiritual and the carnal, especially as delineated by the Church in the culture is touched upon in a blog by James Emory White *(http://Churchand*

culture.org) for January 29, 2015. He wrote, "One of the most glaring divides in the life of many Churches is the divide between principles and practices. A Church might say, "We are a friendly Church. We are warm and welcoming." But five minutes through the doors and it's clear that they are friendly to people they know, friendly to people they like, or simply friendly to people like them. They are not friendly; they are a clique. We throw around words like contemporary, relevant and practical, but seem divorced from what that really means to the person needing it to be contemporary, relevant and practical. We talk of reaching a post-Christian culture, but seem only aware of the Christian sub-culture in which we inhabit. We speak of mission and vision, strategy and DNA, but seem unaware of what ours actually embodies. We talk of conversion growth when we functionally are focused on transfer growth…and reaching the next generation when we are slowly aging out as a body."

His words are a keen analysis of all too many Churches who claim viability without recognizing they have been moving sideways and downward. This direction has been with them for an extended time and they no longer see the real cause and effect for what is occurring internally. All kinds of warnings were issued to God's people in Jeremiah's day but the leaders and the people refused to acknowledge them. They were given direction in terms of the right path they should travel but they refused to listen to the direction. Note what is recorded in Jeremiah 6:13-16 (NIV), "From the least to the greatest, all are greedy for gain; prophets and priests alike, all practice deceit. They dress the wound of my people as though it were not serious. 'Peace, peace,' they say, when there is no peace. Are they ashamed of their detestable conduct? No, they have no shame at all; they do not even know how to blush. So they will fall among the fallen; they will be brought down when I punish them, says the Lord. This is what the Lord says: Stand at the crossroads and look; ask for the ancient paths, ask where the good way is, and walk in it, and you will find rest for your souls. But you said, "We will not walk in it." While standing at the crossroad, with eternal implications in the balance, they preferred and chose the detour and side road rather than the right way.

The article by James Emory White continues:

> So why the seemingly clueless gap between principle and practice? I think there are at least four reasons: (1) We have a natural default mode that we fall into. For example, when it comes to outreach, the default for most is to speak to the already convinced. The power of a principle is that it leads us away from how we might normally act. But if we are not intentional about the principle, we'll go with our natural flow. And our natural flow is not to those outside of our doors, but those who are already inside. (2) We're not serious about the principle. We give lip service to principles because they sound good, make us look good, make us seem on a cutting edge, but it never translates into action (read, change). As a result, we are like a resounding gong or clanging cymbal (I Corinthians 13), or maybe more to the point, hearers of the word only (James 1). (3) We have a terrible blind spot fed by pride. I can't begin to tell you how many times I've heard a leader say, I don't need to spend time on children's ministry. We've got that one down. What I need to know is…. But (as mentioned above) five minutes exposure to their children's ministry, and it's clear they desperately need to spend time on it. Everyone has blind spots but if they are based on pride, they will stay blind spots for a very long time. (4) We've been schooled on various principles, but not on the practices that should follow. This is key. Conferences and books are filled with principles, but you need to see working models, hear actual messages, to really get the practice side of things. You can talk about messages, music and atmospheres being oriented toward the "nones" and "dones" all day long, but it takes seeing it,

feeling it, experiencing it actually happen for a clear picture to form in your mind...Espousing a principle without fleshing it out in practice is no different than having no principles at all.

Because of the dissidence of the people in Jeremiah 6, some very sad words are spoken by the Lord to them (verses 17-19), "I appointed watchmen over you and said, 'Listen to the sound of the trumpet!' But you said, 'We will not listen.' Therefore hear, you nations; you who are witnesses, observe what will happen to them. Hear, you earth: I am bringing disaster on this people, the fruit of their schemes, because they have not listened to my words and have rejected my law." A local visible Church may disagree with the statistics cited earlier and even the words of warning written by Jeremiah, but they cannot disagree with the factualness of them. If a local Church did a self-examination and self-assessment of how things actually are in the Church, they would be able to seek for and apply the remedy. For some of them, they have gotten used to the Highway of Carnality, the detour and side road, and would argue there is no reason to change direction or course. If only they would read and heed God's Words in Jeremiah! If only they would display a willingness and readiness to turn around (repent) and head in God's direction!

One of the major anomalies that occurs when people travel on the wrong highway is indicated in the Parable of the Seed and Sower. As the seed is scattered, there all kinds of soil that are not satisfactory for the seed to germinate and grow. In Mark 4:17-19, there is a description of such a soil and the ensuing impact. The seed spread on the unsatisfactory soil, "But since they have no root, they last only a short time. When trouble or persecution comes because of the word, they quickly fall away. Still others, like seed sown among thorns, hear the word; but the worries of this life, the deceitfulness of wealth and the desires for other things come in and choke the word, making it unfruitful..." The key phrase speaks of the things that stunt any growth - the worries of this life, the deceitfulness of wealth, the desires for other things - all have the capacity of choking the word and causing it to be non-productive.

In Romans 7:14-25, Paul shares his own personal journey and struggle with the standard of God and the susceptibility of one's flesh. His words describe the tension he experienced and endured. He wrote:

> We know that the law is spiritual; but I am unspiritual, sold as a slave to sin. I do not understand what I do. For what I want to do I do not do, but what I hate I do. And if I do what I do not want to do, I agree that the law is good. As it is, it is no longer I myself who do it, but it is sin living in me. For I know that good itself does not dwell in me, that is, in my sinful nature. For I have the desire to do what is good, but I cannot carry it out. For I do not do the good I want to do, but the evil I do not want to do—this I keep on doing. Now if I do what I do not want to do, it is no longer I who do it, but it is sin living in me that does it. So I find this law at work: Although I want to do good, evil is right there with me. For in my inner being I delight in God's law; but I see another law at work in me, waging war against the law of my mind and making me a prisoner of the law of sin at work within me. What a wretched man I am! Who will rescue me from this body that is subject to death?

Do you ever have to cope with the same tensions Paul is describing? You know the right thing God expects of you and inwardly you want to comply. However, the conflict within is telling you that you don't really need to do that which you'd rather not do. Paul categorizes it as, "the evil I do not want to do." It is an obvious spiritual conflict - to sin or not to sin; to do what is right or to do the alternative; to champion the good or succumb to the wrong and bad. Paul describes it as a law that is "waging war against the law of my mind." It gives amplification to what he wrote the Ephesian believers (6:10-13, NIV).

> Finally, be strong in the Lord and in his mighty power. Put on the full armor of God, so that you can take your stand against the devil's schemes. For our struggle is not against flesh and blood, but against the rulers, against the authorities, against the powers of this dark world and against the spiritual forces of evil in the heavenly realms. Therefore put on the full armor of God, so that when the day of evil comes, you may be able to stand your ground, and after you have done everything, to stand.

Paul is indicating that one would be wise to know who the enemy is and the persuasive power of that enemy. The terms he uses regarding the conflict is that "…our struggle is not against flesh and blood, but against the rulers, against the authorities, against the powers of this dark world and against the spiritual forces of evil in the heavenly realms." Even though the enemy is formidable, there is no good reason for us to be willing to surrender to the inevitable. In Romans 7:25, Paul tells us why surrender is never a viable option for us who believe in Jesus Christ. However, we are to lift high our banner that emblazons and enunciates: "Thanks be to God, who delivers us through Jesus Christ our Lord!"

Surprisingly, despite all of this clear guidance and personal example, Paul has to once again address the subject of the flesh and carnality in Romans 8:1-10.

> Therefore, there is now no condemnation for those who are in Christ Jesus, because through Christ Jesus the law of the Spirit who gives life has set you free from the law of sin and death. For what the law was powerless to do because it was weakened by the flesh, God did by sending his own Son in the likeness of sinful flesh to be a sin offering. And so he condemned sin in the flesh, in

order that the righteous requirement of the law might be fully met in us, who do not live according to the flesh but according to the Spirit.

The objective for the professing believer is to live according to the Spirit. Sadly, he must once again caution about those who choose the alternative and follow the dictates of the flesh.

> Those who live according to the flesh have their minds set on what the flesh desires; but those who live in accordance with the Spirit have their minds set on what the Spirit desires. The mind governed by the flesh is death, but the mind governed by the Spirit is life and peace. The mind governed by the flesh is hostile to God; it does not submit to God's law, nor can it do so. Those who are in the realm of the flesh cannot please God.

The comparison is made of the right relationship versus the wrong desires. The difference is whether one is living in the Spirit or living according to the flesh with their mind set on what the flesh desires. If one persists in catering to his fleshly desires, the words concerning him are very descriptive - death; hostility toward God; not submissive to God's law; cannot please God. By contrast, those believers intent on pleasing God and living in the Spirit are those who desire to do what the Spirit desires them to do. When the mind is governed by the Spirit it results in life and peace. Which life do you personally desire, the life in the flesh or the life in the Spirit? Which life do you know for certainty is the life you are now living? Within the context of the 21st Century Church you attend, are these truths waxing or waning in your Church? Are these truths waxing or waning in you?

It is obvious that the culture, rather than the Church, is making greater inroads in one's thinking and practice. It has a much greater impact on laws that are evolving in our nation. The professing believer should be a more bold confessing believer. Do you know which one you are? If in doubt, what do you believe is the wise and right decision for you to make today? A prayer for the Church and individual lives should be:

Spirit of God, descend upon my heart;
Wean it from earth; through all its pulses move;
Stoop to my weakness, mighty as Thou art;
And make me love Thee as I ought to love.

Hast Thou not bid me love Thee, God and King?
All, all Thine own, soul, heart and strength and mind.
I see Thy cross; there teach my heart to cling:
O let me seek Thee, and O let me find!

8. Reclamation and Revitalization

Awaken your might; come and save us. Restore us, O God; make your face shine upon us, that we may be saved. O Lord God Almighty, how long will your anger smolder against the prayers of your people? Restore us, O God Almighty; make your face shine upon us, that we may be saved. Return to us, O God Almighty! Look down from heaven and see! Let your hand rest on the man at your right hand, the son of man you have raised up for yourself. Then we will not turn away from you; revive us, and we will call on your name. Restore us, O LORD God Almighty; make your face shine upon us, that we may be saved.
Psalm 80 (NIV - Selected)

Does the Church and Christian need reclamation, revitalization and revival today? Stephen Olford (1918-2004) was a gifted expositor and author. One of his early writings, *Heart cry For Revival* (1969), challenged and served the Church and the servants of the Lord very well. In it, he shared his passion for the Christian, the Church and the world. There was a response on a special occasion, when he wrote:

> Never was a Church-wide, heaven-sent revival needed than at this present time. It is the only answer to the spiritual warfare we face in every part of the world. Bombs, bullets and body bags will never stem the tide of terror and horror that threatens human existence. We must recognize that 'the weapons of our warfare are not carnal but mighty in God for pulling down strongholds, casting down arguments and every high thing that exalts itself against the knowledge of God, bringing every thought into captivity to the obedience of Christ' (2 Corinthians 10:4-5).

James Perry

In a similar way, Dr. A.W. Tozer (1897-1963) wrote:

> Christianity today is man-centered, not God-centered. God is made to wait patiently, even respectfully, on the whims of men. The image of God currently popular is that of a distracted Father, struggling in heartbroken desperation to get people to accept a Savior of whom they feel no need and in whom they have very little interest. To persuade these self-sufficient souls to respond to His generous offers God will do almost anything, even using salesmanship methods and talking down to them in the chummiest way imaginable.

Dr. Tozer was a man who labored tirelessly to instruct as many as he could in the whole counsel of God. One of the observations he made, despite his best and most diligent efforts was,

Millions call themselves by His name, it is true, and pay some token homage to Him, but a simple test will show how little He is really honored among them. Let the average man be put to the proof on the question of who or what is above, and his true position will be exposed. Let him be forced into making a choice between God and money, between God and men, between God and personal ambition, God and self, God and human love, and God will take second place every time. Those other things will be exalted above. However the man may protest, the proof is in the choice he makes day after day throughout his life.

As difficult as it may be to understand, some individuals will have to sink to the lowest possible state of existence before there is any possibility of coming to one's senses and desiring reclamation and restoration. *The British Dictionary* (http://dictionary.reference.com/browse/reclamation) defines reclamation as: "The conversion of a desert marsh or wasteland into land suitable for cultivation; the recovery of useful substances from waste products; and, the act of reclaiming or state of being claimed." In terms of the human being and human soul, there is the hope and possibility of taking the long journey back to a place where one can be useful once again. One biblical example is the parable of the prodigal son in Luke 15 (ESV). The sad story is told in verses 13-16:

> Not many days later, the younger son gathered all he had and took a journey into a far country, and there he squandered his property in reckless living. And when he had spent everything, a severe famine arose in that country, and he began to be in need. So he went and hired himself out to one of the citizens of that country, who sent him into his fields to feed pigs. And he was longing to be fed with the pods that the pigs ate, and no one gave him anything.

The summary of his life-choice, while clearly stated in these verses, can be narrowed down to a single phrase, "he squandered his property in reckless living" in a strange and distant country.

Once the people who had gathered around him because of the manner in which he behaved and the lavishness of his expenditures, when they realized he had nothing left to spend foolishly on himself and them, they departed and forsook him. The only job anyone would give him was to care for the pigs and to feed them. He sank to the place and status where he was begging to be fed with the pods the pigs were eating. The sad commentary of this bankrupt life and soul at this juncture of his existence was, "no one gave him anything." As he wallowed among the pigs and the swill that was their portion, he thought of a remote but possible alternative to where he was and which he had sunk. Luke 15:17-19 shares his thinking:

> But when he came to himself, he said, How many of my father's hired servants have more than enough bread, but

> I perish here with hunger! I will arise and go to my father, and I will say to him, Father, I have sinned against heaven and before you. I am no longer worthy to be called your son. Treat me as one of your hired servants.

While he had a strategy, he had no idea whether or not his father would look kindly upon this foolish and misguided son. He had not only caused his father grief and a measure of shame, but it caused his father's reputation and prestige to be marred as he sold off some of his land so this demanding son could leave with his inheritance. Some parents might feel very negative toward a wayward child who had squandered valuable assets. It might even cause one to implement the adage, "You made your bed, now sleep in it." However, Luke 15:20-24 tells of the long journey back to his father's home. He has time to think about how he should speak to his father and how his father might react toward him. Note the narrative of these verses:

> And he arose and came to his father. But while he was still a long way off, his father saw him and felt compassion, and ran and embraced him and kissed him. And the son said to him, Father, I have sinned against heaven and before you. I am no longer worthy to be called your son. But the father said to his servants, Bring quickly the best robe, and put it on him, and put a ring on his hand, and shoes on his feet. And bring the fattened calf and kill it, and let us eat and celebrate. For this my son was dead, and is alive again; he was lost, and is found. And they began to celebrate.

The words that stand out are, "His father saw him afar off and felt compassion." The father calls for a celebration. Why? The father gives his response, "This my son was dead, and is alive again; he was lost, and is found." It is obvious that the father spent time longing and looking for this moment of the son's return. While this passage is used in many different ways, it also serves as a lesson and illustration of reclamation, revitalization and revival.

There is a parallel to this text in Ephesians 5:12-17:

> For it is shameful even to speak of the things that they do in secret. But when any-thing is exposed by the light, it becomes visible, for anything that becomes visible is light. Therefore it says, Awake, O sleeper, and arise from the dead, and Christ will shine on you. Look carefully then how you walk, not as unwise but as wise, making the best use of the time, because the days are evil. Therefore do not be foolish, but understand what the will of the Lord is.

A choice is available to everyone at some point in his life. John 1:4-5, 9 (ESV) says, "In Him was life, and the life was the Light of men. The Light shines in the darkness, and the darkness did not comprehend it. The true light, which enlightens everyone, was coming into the world." The true Light pierces the darkness of one's soul and understanding. For the prodigal son, the Light pierced through the muck and mire of the pig sty to penetrate into the dark soul who had wandered so far and for so long. It is the enactment of the words in Ephesians 5, "Awake, O sleeper, and arise from the dead, and Christ will shine on you."

A question for us to ponder and answer is, "How much time do we spend longing and looking for a spiritual awakening in our communities, country and world today?" Do we earnestly desire an outpouring of God's Spirit and for revival to come in our lifetime? What if we echoed the words of Psalm 85:4-8 (ESV), and meant them from the depths of our being. Do we believe God would hear and respond? The prayer would be:

> Restore us again, O God of our salvation, and put away your indignation toward us! Will you be angry with us forever? Will you prolong your anger to all generations? Will you not revive us again, that your people may rejoice in you? Show us your steadfast love, O Lord, and grant us your salvation. Let me hear what God the Lord will speak, for he will speak peace to his people, to his saints; but let them not turn back to folly.

The expression of confidence by the Psalmist that the Lord will hear and respond are seen in the words of verses 9-13.

> Surely his salvation is near to those who fear him, that glory may dwell in our land. Steadfast love and faithfulness meet; righteousness and peace kiss each other. Faithfulness springs up from the ground, and righteousness looks down from the sky. Yes, the Lord will give what is good, and our land will yield its increase. Righteousness will go before him and make his footsteps a way.

Does this represent your longing and expectation? Does this reflect your confidence that the Lord is near to those who fear Him and call upon Him? Do you believe He is eager to hear your heart-cry for revival in this day?

An example for us to consider is the heart-cry of the prophet Habakkuk for reclamation, revitalization and revival is contained within a dialogue that he has with The Lord. It begins with Habakkuk 1:1-4 (NASB).

> The oracle which Habakkuk the prophet saw. How long, O Lord, will I call for help, and You will not hear? I cry out to You, Violence! Yet You do not save. Why do You make me see iniquity, and cause me to look on wickedness? Yes, destruction and violence are before me; strife exists and contention arises. Therefore the law is ignored

and justice is never upheld. For the wicked surround the righteous; therefore justice comes out perverted.

A very distressing and bleak picture is drawn as the Chaldeans advance. They are being used by the Lord to punish Judah. In the midst of the purge, Habakkuk pleads with the Lord for understanding of His rationale for allowing a wicked people to oppress those who are not nearly as wicked. The prophet's plea is expressed in verses 12-13.

> Are You not from everlasting, O Lord, my God, my Holy One? We will not die. You, O Lord, have appointed them to judge; and You, O Rock, have established them to correct. Your eyes are too pure to approve evil, and You cannot look on wickedness with favor. Why do You look with favor on those who deal treacherously? Why are You silent when the wicked swallow up those more righteous than they?

The prophet asserts himself and assumes a posture before The Lord. Habakkuk 2:1-3, is his expression and the Lord's initial response. The prophet states:

> I will stand on my guard post and station myself on the rampart; and I will keep watch to see what He will speak to me, and how I may reply when I am reproved. Then the Lord answered me and said, Record the vision and inscribe it on tablets, that the one who reads it may run. For the vision is yet for the appointed time; it hastens toward the goal and it will not fail. Though it tarries, wait for it; for it will certainly come, it will not delay.

The Lord is indicating that He is aware of their plight and has a perfect plan that will be apparent in His time and manner. Meanwhile, the prophet and the people must wait patiently and endure until the Lord's time-frame is met when His action will be swift and certain. One truth embraced by the prophet, regardless of events and circumstances that occur is, "But the righteous will live by his faith" (Habakkuk 2:4). After pondering the Lord's response and the evidence of His compassion, the prophet offers a prayer, Habakkuk 3:1-2, "Lord, I have heard the report about You and I fear. O Lord, Revive Your work in the midst of the years, in the midst of the years make it known; in wrath remember mercy."

Following the dialogue with the Lord, the book of Habakkuk closes with words of hope, patience, endurance and expectation.

> I heard and my inward parts trembled, at the sound my lips quivered. Decay enters my bones, and in my place I tremble. Because I must wait quietly for the day of distress, for the people to arise who will invade us. Though the fig tree should not blossom and there be no fruit on the vines, though the yield of the olive should fail and the fields produce no food, though the flock should be cut off from the fold and there be no cattle in the stalls, Yet I will exult in the Lord, I will rejoice in the God of my salvation. The Lord God is my strength, and He has made my feet like hinds' feet, and makes me walk on my high places.

Charles H. Spurgeon spoke and wrote often on the subject of reclamation, revitalization and revival. On one occasion, he wrote about personal godliness:

> Urgently do we need a revival of personal godliness. This is, indeed, the secret of Church prosperity. When individuals fall from their steadfastness, the Church is tossed to and fro; when personal faith is steadfast, the Church abides true to her Lord. It is upon the truly godly and spiritual that the future of religion depends in the hand of God. Oh, for more truly holy men, quickened

and filled with the Holy Spirit, consecrated to the Lord and sanctified by His truth. Brethren, we must each one live if the Church is to be alive; we must live unto God if we expect to see the pleasure of the Lord prospering in our hands. Sanctified men are the salt of society and the saviors of the race *(http://spurgeon.org/revival.htm)*.

Similarly, a hymn written in 1779 by John Newton expresses a sense of the heart and mind when one's primary thoughts are not completely upon the Lord. Some of the words of the hymn are:

How tedious and tasteless the hours
When Jesus no longer I see...

O drive these dark clouds from the sky,
Thy soul cheering presence restore...

What are some things we should ponder as we share in the hope and expectation of the prophet? Primarily, it would be beneficial to be thinking upon what God's grace has provided for us. We should be grateful to Him and desire to share with others His truth regarding what it is and means to be redeemed; reclaimed; ransomed; healed; restored and forgiven. We must never forget the riches of His grace to and for us. Also, because of what He has done for us, we ought to be resolved to behave and do those things that would result in glory being given to Him. For some unexplainable reason, there is a prevailing thought where returning to the Lord is made to be more difficult than necessary. Like the prodigal son, a person must come to his senses and make a conscious decision to come humbly back to where he needs to be - in fellowship with his father. It will take determination, humility, perseverance, endurance to begin that journey. It will also consider the possibility of experiencing the father's refusal to embrace the prodigal and the rejection of his prepared plea. None of these things should matter if the person's heart is set on getting right with God the Father and returning into His fold. If there is the commitment and resolve, a person will be able to accept the decision of the Father when the wandering prodigal returns. There are two hymns that come to mind when repentance is the desire. The first is a hymn of commitment that gives expression to what it is to be resolved before the Lord. It was written by James H. Fillmore, Sr. in 1896.

> *I am resolved no longer to linger,*
> *Charmed by the world's delight,*
> *Things that are higher, things that are nobler,*
> *These have allured my sight.*
>
> *I am resolved to go to the Savior,*
> *Leaving my sin and strife...*
>
> *I am resolved to follow the Savior,*
> *Faithful and true each day;*
> *Heed what He sayeth, do what He willeth...*
>
> *Refrain*
>
> *I will hasten to Him, hasten so glad and free;*
> *Jesus, greatest, highest, I will come to Thee.*

The second hymn tells the story of a wandering and straying sheep. During a revival series in a female seminary in Massachusetts (1843), Horatius Bonar felt compelled to pen the words to...

> *I was a wandering sheep, I did not love the fold;*
> *I did not love my Shepherd's voice,*
> *I would not be controlled....*

THE TWENTY-FIRST CENTURY CHURCH:
IS IT WAXING OR WANING

The Shepherd sought His sheep, The Father sought His child;
They followed me o'er vale and hill,
O'er deserts waste and wild…

Jesus my Shepherd is: 'Twas He that loved my soul;
'Twas He that washed me in His blood,
'Twas He that made me whole.
'Twas He that sought the lost,
That found the wand'ring sheep,
'Twas He that brought me to the fold,
'Tis He that still doth keep.

No more a wandering sheep, I love to be controlled;
I love my tender Shepherd's voice, I love the peaceful fold.
No more a wayward child, I seek no more to roam;
I love my heavenly Father's voice, I love, I love His home!

We are numbered with those who have been called by God and been rescued by His grace. Because of His grace alone, we are to be fully committed as the Bride of Jesus Christ. As His Bride (His true Church), He has done particular things to make His Bride to be as He wants her to be before Him. Ephesians 5:24-27 declares, "Christ also loved the Church and gave Himself up for her, so that He might sanctify her, having cleansed her by the washing of water with the word, that He might present to Himself the Church in all her glory, having no spot or wrinkle or any such thing; but that she would be holy and blameless." Jesus Christ wants His Bride to share in His holiness and perfection. It is what He wants to do for you! Because of this work of grace, the invisible Church should be readily visible in us who believe in Him. The invisible Church is to be obviously visible through and by us. This will require the implementation of Romans 12:1-2, present yourselves as a living sacrifice, as we commit ourselves to doing all the will of God for us. There is a meaningful and purposeful prayer of a Pastor for the flock he is shepherding recorded in Colossians 4:12, "Epaphras, who is one of you, a servant of Christ Jesus, greets you, always struggling on your behalf in his prayers, that you may stand mature (perfect) and fully assured in all the will of God."

Our hope is built on nothing less
than Jesus' blood and righteousness...

When Darkness veils his lovely face,
I rest on his unchanging grace...

On Christ the solid rock I stand
all other ground is sinking sand...

9. Calamity of Carnality

> *Therefore there is now no condemnation for those who are in Christ Jesus…For what the Law could not do, weak as it was through the flesh, God did: sending His own Son in the likeness of sinful flesh and as an offering for sin, He condemned sin in the flesh, so that the requirement of the Law might be fulfilled in us, who do not walk according to the flesh but according to the Spirit.*
> *Romans 8:1-9 (Selected - NASB)*

An online dictionary definition for carnal is, "relating to the appetites and passions of the body; sensual; fleshly." There is a clarification and expanded thought under Synonyms *(dictionary.com)* suggesting: "Carnal, although it may refer to the body as opposed to the spirit, often refers to sexual needs or urges: carnal cravings, attractions, satisfactions. Sensual implies a suggestion of eroticism." The Holy Scriptures teach there are only two eternal possibilities for all mankind. There is the possibility of continuing a life that is focused on the fleshly desires and activities or the possibility of living in the Spirit that requires one to be growing in the grace and knowledge of the Lord Jesus Christ. The remaining verses of the reference cited above (Romans 8:1-9) indicate the distinct differences between the two possibilities.

> For those who are according to the flesh set their minds on the things of the flesh, but those who are according to the Spirit, the things of the Spirit. For the mind set on the flesh is death, but the mind set on the Spirit is life and peace, because the mind set on the flesh is hostile toward God; for it does not subject itself to the law of God, for it is not even able to do so, and those who are in the flesh cannot please God. However, you are not in

the flesh but in the Spirit, if indeed the Spirit of God dwells in you. But if anyone does not have the Spirit of Christ, he does not belong to Him.

The idea of the calamity of carnality is based upon a phrase in Romans 8:8, "Those who are in the flesh cannot please God." Calamity is that which causes, "The condition of grievous affliction; misery; deep distress; adversity." Calamity is the result of a person making the inappropriate choices for his life and worldview. Such a one is motivated by self-interests and undisciplined desires. This type person only considers what he wants and when he wants it. He will do whatever is necessary to satisfy his personal urges and desires. The person living in this manner has suppressed his conscience (the searing, desensitizing process) that would dictate right and wrong, good or evil, righteousness or wickedness. Galatians 5:19-21 (NASB) lists particulars that define the carnal appetite: "Now the deeds of the flesh are evident, which are: immorality, impurity, sensuality, idolatry, sorcery, enmities, strife, jealousy, outbursts of anger, disputes, dissensions, factions, envying, drunkenness, carousing, and things like these, of which I forewarn you, just as I have forewarned you, that those who practice such things will not inherit the kingdom of God."

The language of Scripture can be easily understood. The only reason why it may become contorted in particular instances is due to a person's attempt to rationalize away what his behavior is in actuality. Paul began this section by writing, "Now the deeds of the flesh are evident (manifest)." A list then follows indicating that which the Apostle had in his mind about the evident fleshly appetites and desires. When he refers to the flesh, he is not addressing what is visible in the human form but what is hidden within one's human nature. He is indicating the extent and production of the unregenerate and unrenewed human nature. Paul is echoing what Jesus Christ had indicated in an explanation to His disciples about the dietary laws that were being promulgated by the Pharisees. The words of Jesus Christ to His disciples:

> Do you not understand that everything that goes into the mouth passes into the stomach, and is eliminated? But the things that proceed out of the mouth come from the heart, and those defile the man. For out of the heart come evil thoughts, murders, adulteries, fornications, thefts, false witness, slanders. These are the things which defile the man; but to eat with unwashed hands does not defile the man (Matthew 15:17-20).

Jesus and Paul are both indicating that the things the flesh finds pleasing and desirable are well known in the culture. They both indicate that the world is full of illustrations that define the corrupt human nature. These things represent the life of those who have made a mockery of sin (Proverbs 14:9), "Fools mock at making amends for sin.." It is a sad commentary regarding the tendencies of the flesh, as well as the susceptibility of the carnal man. It is a measure of one's character that has been formed by the choices one has made in life.

There are some who believe we are in the last days and standing near the threshold when Jesus Christ will return for His Bride, the Church. This is said out of the context of a world that appears to be spiraling downward at an increasing rate of speed. Even though sin and wickedness are abundant, and even though the courts are legalizing behavior that God has condemned, we can only hope and pray for the Lord's deliverance of His people. When the Psalmist saw a glimpse of the evil and wickedness in his day, Psalm 4:4-5 summarizes his hope and confidence, "You are not a God who takes pleasure in wickedness; No evil dwells with You. The boastful shall not stand before Your eyes; You hate all who do iniquity." That was his assessment and prayer more than three thousand years ago. How long-suffering can we anticipate God will be as He sees the cultural chaos in this period of human history? How much longer will God tolerate the persecution and slaughter of Christians and Jews by radical Islamists? This heart-cry is similar to that which is recorded in Revelation 6:9-11.

> When the Lamb broke the fifth seal, I saw underneath the altar the souls of those who had been slain because of the word of God, and because of the testimony which they had maintained; and they cried out with a loud voice, saying, How long, O Lord, holy and true, will You refrain from judging and avenging our blood on those who dwell on the earth? And there was given to each of them a white robe; and they were told that they should rest for a little while longer, until the number of their fellow servants and their brethren who were to be killed even as they had been, would be completed also.

Our concern should always be aligned with God's sovereign plan for the universe He created. We can inquire in prayer regarding how much longer He will allow wickedness to prevail and increase with impunity. We can wonder before Him in terms of why the righteous have to endure without any legal recourse. The resolve of our hearts should always be: "Your will be done on earth as it is in Heaven" (Matthew 6:10).

We have a glimpse into the mind of God and how He thinks and acts when the children of Israel were in the process of removing the enemy from the Promised Land. God issued certain righteous requirements through Moses. They were clear and precise: "When engaging and destroying an enemy, don't plunder the choice and costly possessions they cherished." We have the scene in Joshua 6 through 8 where it became obvious this requirement had been violated. In summary, a man named Achan coveted some of the precious items and clothing. He took plunder - silver, gold, costly garments - and buried them under his tent. Because of his act, the entire Camp was impacted and affected. God had knowledge of what had been done and who had conceived and carried out this evil. God instructs His people, "There is an accursed thing in your midst, O Israel: you cannot stand until you take away the accursed thing from among you." Achan steps forward and admits what he has done. Achan and his family are ushered out of the Camp. At God's direction, "All Israel stoned Achan with stones and burned everything he had with fire. A great heap of stones was raised over the place to remind people of what happens when people do not obey God." The lesson and witness would be a warning against coveting things and not trusting God to supply for one's needs according to His plan and schedule. The sin of coveting is simply defined as, "To wish, long, or crave for (something, especially the property of another person)."

Similarly, as the Church is being established, there is an incident that brings the swift and powerful action of God in the midst of His people. It is recorded in Acts 5 where we are given insight into the decision when Ananias and his wife Sapphire decided there was a better choice than the one they had made before the Church. They committed themselves to sell some property and to give the proceeds to the emerging and developing Church. When they saw the greater than expected amount they received for their property, they rationalized, coveted and compromised. They withheld a portion for themselves and gave a large amount for the work of the Church. The lesson to be learned here is that any vow made before God is a binding. A person should never renege on a commitment to a Holy God. The basic lesson and instruction is clearly stated in Ecclesiastes 5:1-7 (NIV).

> Guard your steps when you go to the house of God. Go near to listen rather than to offer the sacrifice of fools, who do not know that they do wrong. Do not be quick with your mouth, do not be hasty in your heart to utter anything before God. God is in heaven and you are on earth, so let your words be few…When you make a vow

to God, do not delay in fulfilling it. He has no pleasure in fools; fulfill your vow. It is better not to vow than to make a vow and not fulfill it. Do not let your mouth lead you into sin. And do not protest to the [temple] messenger, My vow was a mistake…Therefore stand in awe of God.

The scene in Acts 5 unfolds when Ananias brings his offering. He is immediately confronted with his deceit and wickedness. The words of Peter must have pierced into the depths of his soul when he heard the words, "You have lied to the Holy Spirit." The Lord struck him dead and his body was carried out. When his wife (widow) arrives, the same confrontation occurs and she also hears the words, "You have lied to the Holy Spirit" and is struck dead because she had connived with her husband to both covet and deceive. They had neglected to take a serious God seriously and suffered the calamity of their carnality. The foundational values of the Church were to represent purity and integrity, not coveting and deception. The application from both incidents, Achan in the Old Testament and Ananias/Sapphire in the New Testament is that commitment and integrity are essential. If either is compromised, rather than the spiritual community waxing (positive and Biblical growth), it will devolve into waning (spiritual decline).

The broader view in terms of the expanding evil and wickedness in the culture and world has been a concern through all generations. The Olivet Discourse of Jesus Christ (Matthew 24 and 25) addresses the response of a Holy God for a world that has rejected Him and become man-focused rather than God-focused. Matthew 24:1-3 (NIV) begins with these words:

> Jesus left the temple and was walking away when his disciples came up to him to call his attention to its buildings. Do you see all these things? He asked. I tell you the truth, not one stone here will be left on another; everyone will be thrown down. As Jesus was sitting on

THE TWENTY-FIRST CENTURY CHURCH: IS IT WAXING OR WANING

the Mount of Olives, the disciples came to him privately. Tell us, they said, when will this happen, and what will be the sign of Your coming and of the end of the age?

Jesus will discuss this with a comparison made regarding the signs and the times as His return nears, with a warning (Verses 4-13).

See to it that no one misleads you. For many will come in My name, saying, I am the Christ, and will mislead many. You will be hearing of wars and rumors of wars. See that you are not frightened, for those things must take place, but that is not yet the end. For nation will rise against nation, and kingdom against kingdom, and in various places there will be famines and earthquakes. But all these things are merely the beginning of birth pangs. Then they will deliver you to tribulation, and will kill you, and you will be hated by all nations because of My name. At that time many will fall away and will betray one another and hate one another. Many false prophets will arise and will mislead many. Because lawlessness is increased, most people's love will grow cold. But the one who endures to the end, he will be saved.

There are questions to consider: Is there religious deception in the world today? Is there an attempt to champion a false god? Are wars and rumors of war current in the world today? Has there been an increase of earthquakes, tornadoes, tsunamis and famine areas in the contemporary world? Is tribulation and persecution occurring anywhere in the world today? Is it increasing and expanding? Are there false prophets surfacing? Are many being misled? Is lawlessness increasing in our day? Is the work of the Church waxing or waning? What are some of the dominant cultural themes today? Are they raising Biblical standards or those that are secular? Despite the presence and increasing influence of these things, Jesus cautions that the end has not yet arrived. His Bride, the Church has a task to carry out for Him (Verse 14), "This gospel of the kingdom shall be preached in the whole world as a testimony to all the nations, and then the end will come." Jesus gives an additional thought regarding the end times in verses 36-42.

> But of that day and hour no one knows, not even the angels of heaven, nor the Son, but the Father alone. For the coming of the Son of Man will be just like the days of Noah. For as in those days before the flood they were eating and drinking, marrying and giving in marriage, until the day that Noah entered the ark, and they did not understand until the flood came and took them all away; so will the coming of the Son of Man be. Then there will be two men in the field; one will be taken and one will be left. Two women will be grinding at the mill; one will be taken and one will be left. Therefore be on the alert, for you do not know which day your Lord is coming.

There is a clear indicator stated by Jesus Christ, "Just like the days of Noah." We should consider what was going on in the days of Noah. To do so, Genesis 6 through 9 gives the conditions that were prevailing in those days. The message and messenger of righteousness was mocked and scorned; the ark building was ridiculed; the warning of rain and a flood was laughed at; and Noah's best efforts were ignored. To better understand, "Just like the days of Noah," it is valuable to consider the scope and intensity of the cultural behavior while Noah was preaching and building.

> Now it came about, when men began to multiply on the face of the land, and daughters were born to them, that the sons of God saw that the daughters of men were beautiful; and they took wives for themselves, whomever they chose. Then the Lord said, My Spirit shall not strive

with man forever, because he also is flesh...Then the Lord saw that the wickedness of man was great on the earth, and that every intent of the thoughts of his heart was only evil continually. The Lord was sorry that He had made man on the earth, and He was grieved in His heart. The Lord said, I will blot out man whom I have created from the face of the land, from man to animals to creeping things and to birds of the sky; for I am sorry that I have made them. (Genesis 6:1-7)

The key phrase to note is, "The wickedness of man was great on the earth, and that every intent of the thoughts of his heart was only evil continually." There is no detailed description given regarding their deeds that were deemed wickedness. The only picture we get of the wickedness is that it was great and all-encompassing upon the earth. Additionally, the thought life of the people was continually evil. It is difficult to imagine the actions that are deemed by God to be great wickedness and the thought-life that is deemed continually evil. The MSG phrases it, "God saw that human evil was out of control. People thought evil, imagined evil from morning to night." The text is referencing the total collapse of moral values and foundational principles that were established by God. Corruption was extensive and perversion had spread like a cancer across the population. It was a time when the words in Romans 3:10-12 (NIV) was the reality during all of Noah's days. The verses indicate: "There is no one righteous, not even one; there is no one who understands, no one who seeks God. All have turned away, they have together become worthless; there is no one who does good, not even one." It was at this point of time, amid this reality when God determined the human race was totally depraved, hopelessly beyond remedy and wickedness was the preference for all the people all of the time.

The Lord was so repulsed by what mankind was doing that it caused him to have regret and sorrow for having created man and the emergence of the human race, Genesis 6:6-7 (NIV) allows us an insight into the heart of God. His reaction and response was: "The Lord was grieved that he had made man on the earth, and his heart was filled with pain. So the Lord said, I will wipe mankind, whom I have created, from the face of the earth--men and animals, and creatures that move along the ground, and birds of the air--for I am grieved that I have made them." Can we begin to imagine God the Creator being "grieved and His heart filled with pain" because of mankind's sin and rejection of Him? If this principle was applied to the current state of the world and culture, how close are we to causing our God to be "grieved and His heart filled with pain" because of the way He and His Word have been rejected and His standards trampled underfoot? Are we arriving at God's threshold point where His grief and pain will result in His judgment and wrath being poured out upon the earth? Have we as a culture and world become identified the dames as in Noah's day?

Some indicators demonstrating that which repulses a serious God is: the unimpeded abortion rate; the legalization of mood modifiers (marijuana is the first step); the LGBT (Lesbian, Gay, Bisexual, Transgender) inroads and the legalization of same gender marriages; the continued legal representations and successes of the atheistic proponents; pedophilia and pornography within the Church at large and the increasing numbers of men addicted to everything from child pornography and into illicit adult relationships; the worldwide increase of persecution toward Christians and Jews - these and other areas are issues for and among professing Christian people. The statistics regarding these behaviors and carnal activities (according to surveys conducted in 2004 and again in 2014 by reputable organizations) have actually increased in the last decade. An organization, Proven Men Ministries along with the George Barna Group, have observed the percentage of pornography addiction is a constant among the various age groups. People would be shocked by the statistical findings where 77% of men in two distinct age groups look at pornography at least monthly. One reputable organization's survey of Pastors and Ministers discovered that a large percentage (slightly more than 50%) were tempted and had yielded to observing some form of pornography. The surveys do not ask the men (or women) why pornography or the erotic have such appeal and attraction for them.

Women are also attracted to and consumed by the erotic. A recent book, *Fifty Shades of Grey*, is discussed in a critique appearing on the website of *ChurchLeaders.com* entitled, "Fifty Ways Porn Might Be Sneaking into Your Church" by, Dannah Gresh. A summary statement of the influence this book may have in the reader's life and mental voyeurisms is: "Fifty Shades of Grey is classified as erotic fiction. According to one online dictionary *(http://www.merriam-webster.com/dictionary/erotic)*, this genre of literature is defined as that which has no literary or artistic value other than to stimulate sexual desire." The result from reading this book is the comment of a woman who said she, "Can't get the images out of her head." For many years, on both radio and television, there is programming that was called Soap Operas (so called because they were sponsored by laundry soap and detergent companies). An appeal to this programming is the demonstration of the complex and complicated romantic relationships than can and do exist.

Within the Church and the professing Christian community, why has there been an ignoring of and departure from the standards of God that require His people to follow another course for their lives?

> Do not love the world or anything in the world. If anyone loves the world, the love of the Father is not in him. For everything in the world--the cravings of sinful man, the lust of his eyes and the boasting of what he has and does--comes not from the Father but from the world. The world and its desires pass away, but the man

who does the will of God lives forever" (I John 2:15-17, NIV)?

Why is it that so many have chosen a path other than the one stated in Psalm 1:1-2 (NIV)?

> Blessed is the man who does not walk in the counsel of the wicked or stand in the way of sinners or sit in the seat of mockers. But his delight is in the law of the Lord, and on His law he meditates day and night?

Why is it that in this same Psalm (verses 3-6) so many have allowed themselves to follow an alternative path where their fellow-travelers are those who will perish? The verses are precise regarding the pathway of the righteous and that of the wicked.

> He (the righteous) is like a tree planted by streams of water, which yields its fruit in season and whose leaf does not wither. Whatever he does prospers. Not so the wicked! They are like chaff that the wind blows away. Therefore the wicked will not stand in the judgment, nor sinners in the assembly of the righteous. For the Lord watches over the way of the righteous, but the way of the wicked will perish.

Where is the right and safe place for the Church and professing Christian to be amid the cultural chaos of our day? Do you find your pleasure in things that are spiritual or things that are decadent? Wherever you are located in this world, is your Christian life waxing or waning? Is the Church you attend waxing or waning? It should matter to you because it most assuredly matters to God. You can and must avoid the calamity of carnality. Let the prayer of your heart be in the words of the Hymn (and Psalm 139:23-24):

THE TWENTY-FIRST CENTURY CHURCH: IS IT WAXING OR WANING

Search me, O God, And know my heart today;
Try me, O Savior, Know my thoughts, I pray.
See if there be Some wicked way in me;
Cleanse me from every sin And set me free.
J. Edwin Orr (1936)

Search me, O God, and know my heart;
test me and know my thoughts.
Point out anything in me that offends you,
and lead me along the path of everlasting life.
Psalm 139:23-24 (NLT)

10. Escaping the Grip of Carnality

Do this, knowing the time, that it is already the hour for you to awaken from sleep; for now salvation is nearer to us than when we believed. The night is almost gone, and the day is near. Therefore let us lay aside the deeds of darkness and put on the armor of light. Let us behave properly as in the day, not in carousing and drunkenness, not in sexual promiscuity and sensuality, not in strife and jealousy. But put on the Lord Jesus Christ, and make no provision for the flesh in regard to its lusts.
Romans 13:11-14 (NASB)

The previous chapter dealt with the calamity of carnality and the consequences when the carnal mind and things of the flesh become the dominant desire of one's life. Not only does it make one a captive to evil and wickedness, but mankind, committed to carnal living, brings regret and pain to the heart of The Creator. One of the sadder realities is the subtle attacks and victories of our enemy, the devil, and how easily good people succumb to this wily manner and ways. The subtle approach will always be in the area of one's greatest vulnerability. In a conversation I was having with my son who is a lay-leader in his Church, he shared the passion of his heart and commitment when he said, "Dad - if people would only read their Bible - just the Bible - what a difference it would make in their lives and life choices." He is absolutely correct! The context of our conversation was in terms of the choices and compromises that occur when someone does not faithfully adhere to what God has said. For those who are oriented to Catechetical memorization and instruction, Question and Answer #3 of the *Westminster Shorter Catechism* is: "What do the scriptures principally teach? The scriptures principally teach what man is to believe concerning God, and what duty God requires of man." The more faithfully one reads the Scriptures and meditates upon them, the more he will understand what he is to believe about God and His kingdom. Additionally, he will also learn those duties required of those who believe in Him and who seek to honor His Word.

It is especially grievous when men who preach the Word allow compromises and rationalizations to become their practice of religion. The methods of operation begin to reflect more of one who has become culture-oriented within the secular society rather being enraptured with those who are members of the invisible Church, the Bride of Jesus Christ. This is the great divide and place where life choices need sharper definition. Will the cultural values be followed for personal purposes and conveniences or will spiritual values be the consistent basis for the decisions one makes and the actions one takes? What is required of one who bears the name of Jesus Christ and identifies himself as a Christian? It is disconcerting when those who should know and do better allow themselves to breach ethical lines for personal advantage or gain. An example of this is reported in *World Magazine*, February 21, 2015, with an article by Warren Cole Smith on "Buying a bestseller." It appears in the Religion Section and asks: "Is David Jeremiah another gifted pastor who has used what some say is an ethically dubious method to promote books?" How will a gifted person respond? What will his rationalization and justification be as his response? In the context of the article, the following is noted: "No single event brought down Seattle's Mars Hill Church and its celebrity pastor Mark Driscoll. However, the revelation that Driscoll and the Church used nearly $250,000 in Church funds to buy one of Driscoll's books onto *The New York Times* bestseller list was a key factor. Gaming *The New York Times* bestseller list is not illegal, but Justin Taylor at Crossway Books called the practice, "dishonoring to the Lord." Dan Busby, president of the Evangelical Council for Financial Accountability (ECFA), calls it "unethical," and ECFA adopted a rule against members in good standing engaging in it. Rick Christian, a literary agent who founded *Alive Communications* in 1989, calls such practices

THE TWENTY-FIRST CENTURY CHURCH: IS IT WAXING OR WANING

"outright fraud" and says, "Let's quit sugar-coating bad practices, quit looking the other way, quit justifying complicit involvement because others are doing it." He calls for rules of conduct "every agent, publisher, agency, Church, and ministry should sign off on." Pastor and author David Jeremiah seems to disagree. According to former employee George Hale, Jeremiah's ministry, Turning Point, purchased copies of at least three of Jeremiah's books to push them onto *The New York Times* bestseller list. *World Magazine* asked Jeremiah about his book marketing practices in an interview last year. He was vague on the specifics but did say, "You can't just write a book and say I'm not going to have anything to do with marketing. If you don't care enough about it to try and figure out how to get it in the hands of other people, nobody else is going to either." Marketing has certainly been successful for Jeremiah and Turning Point. The ministry has doubled in size since 2007, at a time when—because of the Great Recession—many Christian ministries have struggled to maintain their donor bases and break even. In 2012, the ministry took in about $40 million… *World Magazine* placed dozens of calls to David Jeremiah and other members of the Turning Point staff to confirm Hale's version of events and to give Jeremiah the opportunity to explain his version of events. None of these calls were returned.

It is a sad and grievous day when good men allow themselves to resort to doing things man's way rather than God's way. At issue is whether or not one's actions and ethics bring dishonor and reproach to the name and cause of the Lord Jesus Christ. If one gets onto the road of the cultural-oriented, is there any easy possibility of escaping from the grip of carnality (that which pertains to or characterized by the flesh or the body, its passions and appetites; sensual; carnal pleasures; not spiritual; merely human; temporal; worldly)? Once anyone places himself on that pathway he becomes somewhat resolute and defensive. He sets himself up by becoming obstinate, resolute and not open to correction or change. An attitude ensues that projects, "I know what I am doing and why I am doing it." This attitude and posture becomes a barrier to consideration for an alternative course one should be following. This type of resolute stance is seen in the defensive rationalization of David Jeremiah quoted in the above article, "You can't just write a book and say I'm not going to have anything to do with marketing. If you don't care enough about it to try and figure out how to get it in the hands of other people, nobody else is going to either." This is a case of "the end justifying the means" secular philosophy of life. If God wants one to have a best-seller book, is He not capable of bringing that result to pass? Is personal pride at the root of wanting to have one's writings widely circulated? Is it a latent desire to be popular and widely recognized as one's writings are classified as being a best-seller? Why has one written and published a book? Is it done for the honor and glory of Jesus Christ or for acclaim to be given to a man?

The introductory verses from Romans 13 at the beginning of this chapter contain the directive for a victorious Christian life, "Make no provision for the flesh in regard to its lusts." With that being said, there are several warnings given to the Biblical Christian regarding the reality of an enemy who would seek to undermine one in whatever stratagem accomplishes his diabolical goals. In a day when the Church was under political and secular attack, Peter warned and cautioned the people of his day and their need for vigilance. The reason is that the enemy has many schemes and subtleties that he will employ to ruin or destroy the Christian. His attempts today are no similar to when he thought the cross and the crucifixion of Jesus Christ would bring an end to the Kingdom of God. His greatest attempt and effort was thwarted when the day of resurrection occurred and resulted in victory and triumph over death and hell. Peter did his utmost to prepare those with whom he was ministering of what they were to remember and resist. His words of encouragement to the believers in I Peter 5:6-11 should be noted and implemented.

THE TWENTY-FIRST CENTURY CHURCH: IS IT WAXING OR WANING

> Therefore humble yourselves under the mighty hand of God, that He may exalt you at the proper time, casting all your anxiety (care) on Him, because He cares for you. Be of sober spirit, be on the alert. Your adversary, the devil, prowls around like a roaring lion, seeking someone to devour. But resist him, firm in your faith, knowing that the same experiences of suffering are being accomplished by your brethren who are in the world. After you have suffered for a little while, the God of all grace, who called you to His eternal glory in Christ, will Himself perfect, confirm, strengthen and establish you. To Him be dominion forever and ever. Amen!

Those within the framework of the cultural-oriented Church can benefit from the historical setting and the sobering words of Peter. There is an enemy whose mission is to devour. A brief synopsis of the craftiness and objective of the enemy indicates he will resort to any means to deceive and ensnare a professing Christian. Jesus spoke of him as a murderer and liar (John 8:44). Paul spoke of the enemy as being other than mere flesh and blood. To resist any onslaught by the enemy, the professing Christian was instructed to put on the entire armor of God so he would be enabled to stand amid the evil day and all onslaughts (Ephesians 6). In II Thessalonians 2:6-11, we have a grim and graphic picture of the enemy's actions.

> For the mystery of lawlessness is already at work; only he who now restrains will do so until he is taken out of the way. Then that lawless one will be revealed whom the Lord will slay with the breath of His mouth and bring to an end by the appearance of His coming; that is, the one whose coming is in accord with the activity of Satan, with all power and signs and false wonders, and with all the deception of wickedness for those who perish, because they did not receive the love of the truth so as to

be saved. For this reason God will send upon them a deluding influence so that they will believe what is false, in order that they all may be judged who did not believe the truth, but took pleasure in wickedness.

There are many ways and areas where one is susceptible to the wiles of the enemy. In the unguarded moment, he will subtlety undermine, erode one's faith values, ensnare or frontally attack the unexacting and under-prepared Christian. The previous chapter briefly addressed the susceptibility among men in the area of pornography (we also noted the erotic sensations women receive through some "Soap Operas" and reading or viewing material such as, *Fifty Shades of Gray*). An advertisement appearing in *World Magazine*, February 21, 2015 edition employs a headline that states, "Why 68% of Christian men watch porn." The sub-title adds: "A new generation of porn addicts is about to flood the Church - are we ready?" The advertisement article is written by Terry Cu-Unjieng who asks: "Are we really supposed to buy into the idea that 68% of men in Church watch porn regularly? Could this just be sensational rhetoric? Not according to a national survey among Churches. The survey conducted over the past five years revealed that 68% of Christian men and 50% of pastors view pornography regularly. But even more shocking is that 11-17 year-old boys reported being its greatest users. The Church is in the sexual battle or its life." The survey was conducted by Pure Desire Ministries and the data was contained in "Porn Usage in Evangelical Churches - 2009."

This is a constant and accelerating undermining in a person's life and character across all age groups. It is subtle but it accomplishes the victimization of the Christian and renders him to be preoccupied with sensual rather than spiritual considerations. It causes one to ignore the basic considerations of Psalm 1; Blessed is the man who (1) walks not in the counsel of the ungodly, (2) Who does not pause or hesitate along the pathway of the sinner and those sinning, and (3) Who does not allow himself to sit down with the wicked and those who seek to

THE TWENTY-FIRST CENTURY CHURCH: IS IT WAXING OR WANING

repudiate God and His Word. We should review and asks ourselves frequently, "Is my spiritual life waxing or waning? As a servant of the Lord in His Church, does my attitude and propensity toward the carnal cause a particular Church to be waxing or waning?"

The points in Psalm 1 were vivid on an occasion when some of us gathered in New Orleans, LA for a Church denominational meeting (a Presbytery Meeting). A friend and former classmate wanted to see the French Quarter. He asked if I would drive him there so we could walk in that area and then return to our motel. Dan and I drove there and one of the first available parking spaces was near Bourbon Street. We parked and decided to walk to the French Quarter and back again. As we walked down Bourbon Street, we paused to watch some children dancing in the street. However, that was not all that was visible. The further we walked the more obvious it became that we were in the wrong place. Almost simultaneously, Dan and I uttered similar words that amounted to, "We don't belong here…let's find our way back to where we parked the car." We did that briskly. Even with a brisk stride, we were in visible proximity to the over-drugged and the overtly under-clothed. We both commented how "dirty" we felt because of our brisk walk through the environs of the ungodly and where wickedness was easily accessible.

It is certain that this is how addictions to various matters begin and gain a grasp upon the Christian. It is the grasp of carnality that should be avoided and from which one must find a way of escape. In the *CIU* (Columbia International University) *Today*, Winter 2015, there is an article entitled, "Samson's Promise" by Bob Holmes. The group identifies with the biblical Samson and how easily he became prey for the subtle approach of a very attractive and sexually oriented woman. Even though Samson had taken the Law of the Nazarite Vow, which forbade certain behaviors and indulgences, he succumbed to his attraction to Delilah. His yielding to temptation resulted in his immediate demise and being ensnared in the grasp of carnality. The author of The Samson's Promise article is one who became enticed and addicted to pornography at a young age. He writes:

> The experience of viewing pornography is similar to the experience of taking a drug. Chemicals are released in the brain. The heart rate increases and your adrenaline spikes. Pornography is a plague that spreads quickly and thoroughly. When I enrolled in CIU in the fall of 2010, I heard about this group called Samson's Promise advertised during a single men's chapel. Samson's Promise is a group that is devoted to helping men find victory over sexual sin. We read a book that addresses our challenges. This year we are working through a very well-known Christian book dealing with victory over sexual sin: *Every Man's Battle* by Stephen Arterburn and Fred Stoeker. We read a section of the book and then we come together once a week as our leader guides us through questions based on that chapter. The questions are designed to spark lots of open and honest discussion. The key to a successful accountability group is a commitment to openness and honesty. Without openness the group would be pointless. My experience with Samson's Promise has been a great one. It encourages men to be intentional in developing relationships of accountability with other believing men. You need to know that you are not alone, and you need to be aggressive in this battle for control of your life.

There are basic truths that should be an anchor for one's soul and meditated upon frequently. As an encouragement for the one wishing to escape from the grip of carnality, Hebrews 4:14-16 (NIV) shares these purposeful words.

> Therefore, since we have a great high priest who has ascended into heaven, Jesus the Son of God, let us hold

firmly to the faith we profess. For we do not have a high priest who is unable to empathize with our weaknesses, but we have one who has been tempted in every way, just as we are—yet he did not sin. Let us then approach God's throne of grace with confidence, so that we may receive mercy and find grace to help us in our time of need.

When the enemy seeks to probe an area of vulnerability in your life, do you approach God's throne of grace and mercy confidently? If you do, His mercy and grace will gush out from His throne in your time of need. It will result in spiritual maturation as you experience waxing rather than waning in your life's values and choices.

Additionally, I Corinthians 10:1-13 (NIV) is a powerful passage regarding God's purpose for man and man's propensity to secularize that which should be spiritual in his life and commitment. Some of the statements in this passage are:

> Our ancestors were all under the cloud and they all passed through the sea…They all ate the same spiritual food and drank the same spiritual drink; for they drank from the spiritual rock that accompanied them, and that rock was Christ. Nevertheless, God was not pleased with most of them; their bodies were scattered in the wilderness. Now these things occurred as examples to keep us from setting our hearts on evil things as they did. Do not be idolaters…or indulge in revelry. We should not commit sexual immorality…We should not test Christ…do not grumble, as some of them did and were killed by the destroying angel. These things happened to them as examples and were written down as warnings for us…So, if you think you are standing firm, be careful that you don't fall! No temptation has overtaken you except what is common to mankind. And God is

faithful; he will not let you be tempted beyond what you can bear. But when you are tempted, He will also provide a way out so that you can endure it.

Do these words describe you in any way? Do you indulge in behaviors that are contrary to God's will and purpose for you? Do you test God with your attitude and life management choices? Do you grumble and become annoyed when He ignores your selfish choices and keeps prodding you to do that which will honor Him?
When you reach the point where you are willing to forsake the path you have chosen and are ready to be and do God's best will and purpose for your life, there are meaningful, caring and encouraging words from Him for you.

> You are my servant, I have chosen you and not cast you off, fear not, for I am with you; be not dismayed, for I am your God; I will strengthen you, I will help you, I will uphold you with my righteous right hand…I, the Lord your God, hold your right hand; it is I who say to you, Fear not, I am the one who helps you. (Isaiah 41:9-13, ESV)

Additionally, the words in Isaiah 43:1-5 (ESV) are also for you who have yielded your all to Him.

> But now thus says the Lord, He who created you…He who formed you…Fear not, for I have redeemed you; I have called you by name, you are mine. When you pass through the waters, I will be with you; and through the rivers, they shall not overwhelm you; when you walk through fire you shall not be burned, and the flame shall not consume you. For I am the Lord your God, the Holy One…your Savior…you are precious in my eyes, and honored, and I love you…Fear not, for I am with you…

THE TWENTY-FIRST CENTURY CHURCH: IS IT WAXING OR WANING

Why would any sensible person choose to ignore the faithful God Who pours out His love and redemption upon His people? If you are truly His, why would you choose to repudiate His Word in any way or at any time by your self-management and lifestyle preferences? Have you genuinely escaped the grip of carnality in your life? If not now, when? If not here, where?

Nevertheless, I am continually with You; You hold my right hand. You guide me with your counsel, and afterward You will receive me to glory. Whom have I in heaven but You? And there is nothing on earth that I desire besides You. My flesh and my heart may fail, but God is the strength of my heart and my portion forever. it is good for me to be near God; I have made the Lord God my refuge, that I may tell of all Your works.
Psalm 73:23-28 (ESV Selected)

11. Enculturated or Enraptured?

If the world hates you, you know that it has hated Me before it hated you. If you were of the world, the world would love its own; but because you are not of the world, but I chose you out of the world, because of this the world hates you. Remember the word that I said to you, 'A slave is not greater than his master.' If they persecuted Me, they will also persecute you; if they kept My word, they will keep yours also. But all these things they will do to you for My name's sake, because they do not know the One who sent Me.
John 15:15-21 (NASB)

Jesus is very clear that the distinguishing mark that separates the enculturated (to change, modify, or adapt to the culture) from the enraptured (to fill with delight in Christ, spiritual things) is one's relationship to the world. The world will infiltrate the Church at every opportunity so that the Church's message and impact will be diminished. Getting ensnared by the world's standards and allowing oneself to be taken into the grip of carnality is a very serious matter. Some of the reasons for the presence of the carnal and worldly influences to permeate the visible Church are a declaration made by the Apostle Paul in I Corinthians 3:1-4 (NIV).

> Brothers and sisters, I could not address you as people who live by the Spirit but as people who are still worldly—mere infants in Christ. I gave you milk, not solid food, for you were not yet ready for it. Indeed, you are still not ready. You are still worldly. For since there is jealousy and quarreling among you, are you not worldly? Are you not acting like mere humans? For when one says, I follow Paul, and another, I follow Apollos, are you not mere human beings?

Obviously, Paul is showing the distinction between that which is "worldly" versus that which should be "godly" and present in the visible Church. Many times, it is a determined minority who will agitate and demand their way within the visible Church. The idea of "submission to one another" and the prescribed guideline how Christians should interact with each other within the visible Church is usually ignored. There is the presence of those who bear bridges and resentment toward others. There are some who harbor deep-rooted bitterness. There are those present who negatively influence ministry so that a spirit of rivalry, resentment and division occurs. They seem to be uninhibited, unrestrained and seldom challenged. It festers and is a cause of a particular Church waning rather than waxing! For the cultural-oriented within the Church, the words of Jeremiah 6:13-15 (NLT) should be read and applied so that repentance will occur and God's judgment be averted.

> From the least to the greatest, their lives are ruled by greed. From prophets to priests, they are all frauds. They offer superficial treatments for my people's mortal wound. They give assurances of peace when there is no peace. Are they ashamed of their disgusting actions? Not at all—they don't even know how to blush! Therefore, they will lie among the slaughtered. They will be brought down when I punish them, says the Lord.

Consider the more ideal interaction for the visible Church in Ephesians 5:15-21 (NASB).

> Be careful how you walk, not as unwise men but as wise, making the most of your time, because the days are evil. So then do not be foolish, but understand what the will of the Lord is…be filled with the Spirit, speaking to one another in psalms and hymns and spiritual songs, singing and making melody with your heart to the Lord; always giving thanks for all things in the name of our Lord Jesus

THE TWENTY-FIRST CENTURY CHURCH: IS IT WAXING OR WANING

Christ to God, even the Father; and be subject to one another in the fear of Christ.

How does the worldly (cultural-oriented) enter the visible Church? Why is this orientation allowed to become that which dominates the ministry? Can godliness be present when worldliness is dominant within a Church? There is an answer given in James 4:1-10 (ESV).

> What causes quarrels and what causes fights among you? Is it not this, that your passions are at war within you? You desire and do not have, so you murder. You covet and cannot obtain, so you fight and quarrel. You do not have, because you do not ask. You ask and do not receive, because you ask wrongly, to spend it on your passions. You adulterous people! Do you not know that friendship with the world is enmity with God? Therefore whoever wishes to be a friend of the world makes himself an enemy of God. Or do you suppose it is to no purpose that the Scripture says, He yearns jealously over the spirit that he has made to dwell in us? But he gives more grace. Therefore it says, God opposes the proud, but gives grace to the humble. Submit yourselves therefore to God. Resist the devil, and he will flee from you. Draw near to God, and he will draw near to you. Cleanse your hands, you sinners, and purify your hearts, you double-minded. Be wretched and mourn and weep. Let your laughter be turned to mourning and your joy to gloom. Humble yourselves before the Lord, and he will exalt you.

The obvious question is: Is the visible Church ready and willing to deal with the Achan, Ananias and Sapphira attitudes and disobedience within the community of believers? The words above are not just a suggestion or a passing thought. They are a value judgment being revealed to the visible Church by the triune God. If the visible Church does not respond, the final epitaph will be: "Do you not know that friendship with the world is enmity with God? Therefore whoever wishes to be a friend of the world makes himself an enemy of God." Being an "enemy of God" should give everyone pause and cause us all to tremble in the presence of the Holy God as we seek His forgiveness and restoration.

Even though the visible Church will never be perfect, it can be better than what it is and allowed itself to become. Not everyone will be supportive of seeking after godliness. Paul indicates this to Timothy when he wrote a pastoral letter to him. In II Timothy 4:9-16, he stated how lonely taking a decisive stand can be.

> Do your best to come to me quickly, for Demas, because he loved this world, has deserted me and has gone to Thessalonica…Alexander the metalworker did me a great deal of harm. The Lord will repay him for what he has done. You too should be on your guard against him, because he strongly opposed our message. At my first defense, no one came to my support, but everyone deserted me…

It requires fearlessness, fortitude, faithfulness, courage and boldness to be a David who is willing to confront and face the giant Goliath (I Samuel 17). Godly character is forged by commitment and sacrifice to know, learn and do God's perfect will (Romans 12:1-2). The Holy Spirit was leading Paul to leave Ephesus and go to Jerusalem.

> And now, compelled by the Spirit, I am going to Jerusalem, not knowing what will happen to me there. I only know that in every city the Holy Spirit warns me that prison and hardships are facing me. However, I consider my life worth nothing to me; my only aim is to

finish the race and complete the task the Lord Jesus has given me—the task of testifying to the good news of God's grace. (Acts 20:22-24, NIV)

If the Holy Spirit warned you that prison and hardships are facing you, what would you do? Would you stay in your comfort zone and safer place? Would you try to find a hiding place? Would the fear of man's threats override your fear of God's directive to be where He wants you to be and to do what He wants you to do? Would you remain cultural-oriented? Would you persist in waning rather than waxing spiritually?

There will always be laggards and naysayers. These are people who act as though they know more because their personal worldview has become cultural-oriented. They can always see the cup half empty and rarely do they see it half full. They see things only from their vantage point of what can and will work rather than from God's vantage point that the things impossible for man are possible with God. There is a great lesson to be learned from the account where a young rich man comes running to see Jesus. Mark 10:17-27 (ESV) records the incident and how Jesus responds to him. The young man's question is, "Good Teacher, what must I do to inherit eternal life?" Jesus states part of the Ten Commandments in His response. The rich young man believed that he had been properly trained and had attempted to live up to the demands of The Law. The young man said to him, "Teacher, all these I have kept from my youth." Jesus cuts to the chase when He states: "You lack one thing: go, sell all that you have and give to the poor, and you will have treasure in heaven; and come, follow me." This is not the response the young man desired to hear. We detect that from his response and action: "Disheartened by the saying, he went away sorrowful, for he had great possessions." Jesus had measured his sincerity, intent and heart. Would the young man be willing to dispose of everything he possessed so he could gain eternal life? The second part of what Jesus was requiring was, are you ready to come and follow Me? As the man departed, disheartened and sorrowful, Jesus turned and said to His disciples: "How difficult it will be for those who have wealth to enter the kingdom of God!"

The laggards and naysayers rarely see things the way Jesus sees them. Their value system is influenced more by secular standards than by those that are spiritual. Even the disciples were amazed at what they had seen and the remark Jesus shared with them. Jesus knew their thinking just as he knows your thinking about such matters. We read that: "Jesus said to them again, Children, how difficult it is to enter the kingdom of God! It is easier for a camel to go through the eye of a needle than for a rich person to enter the kingdom of God." The response of the disciples is similar to that which is offered by today's laggards and naysayers in the visible Church: "They were exceedingly astonished, and said to him, Then who can be saved?" The disciples received the word that the visible Church needs to embrace and allow it to resonate today: "Jesus looked at them and said, With man it is impossible, but not with God. For all things are possible with God." Do you understand and believe that the Immutable (Unchanging) God is still able to do the impossible today? Do you believe this unequivocally? Are you free from your personal doubt and reservations?

There are two references in God's Word that each of us should embrace and apply in our lives. The first pertains to gaining wisdom in terms of God and what He is able to do. James 1:5-8 (ESV) states: "But if any of you lacks wisdom, let him ask of God, who gives to all generously and without reproach, and it will be given to him." All of us need to know more regarding the mind and will of God. How often do we come to Him with pure motives to ask Him for wisdom? The proviso for how one is to come and ask is, "He must ask in faith without any doubting..." When I was a boy, our Grandmother Isabella, who had come to this country from Scotland, lived with us until her death. She was not only well-versed in the Scriptures, but she also had keen perception and several pithy comments about different matters. She would sometimes ask us, "Children, where did you go and what did you do?" I anticipated that question and that gave me time to concoct an answer that I thought was plausible. When Grandma Isabella heard my response, on more than one occasion, she responded with her Scottish brogue ("I hae me dewbts"): "I have my doubts about that." Is it possible that when we come to God to ask for wisdom that our approach contains the element of, I have my doubts that He will grant it? The difficulty that follows for the one with any degree of doubt is: "The one who doubts is like the surf of the sea, driven and tossed by the wind." The storm-tossed sea is unpredictable and contains all kinds of objects that will wash ashore. The picture is vivid for the person who prays but has doubts that it will accomplish anything. That possibility becomes that person's reality. The text continues: "For that man ought not to expect that he will receive anything from the Lord, being a double-minded man, unstable in all his ways." What a bleak and frightening assessment for the one who is deemed to be unstable and double-minded. The NLT renders verses 7-8: "Such people should not expect to receive anything from the Lord. Their loyalty is divided between God and the world, and they are unstable in everything they do."

The second reference, Ephesians 3:20-21 (ESV), dovetails nicely with James 1. The verses should be employed to enable us to remind ourselves of God's reality in and for our lives. If we relegated it to the category of it being a "nice Benediction," then we would miss the literalness and implication of the words for us. Note them carefully.

> Now to him who is able to do far more abundantly than all that we ask or think, according to the power at work within us, to him be glory in the Church and in Christ Jesus throughout all generations, forever and ever. Amen!

There is no room for doubt with the purposeful and meaningful words, "to him who is able to do far more abundantly than all that we ask or think." Verse 20 in The MSG renders it: "God can do anything, you know, far more than you could ever imagine or guess or request in your wildest dreams! He does it not by pushing us around but by working within us, his Spirit deeply and gently within us." This is also included in II Corinthians 9:8 (NIV), "God is able to bless you abundantly, so that in all things at all times, having all that you need, you will abound in every good work."

Some of the lyric to the song, "Till The Storm Passes" by Charlotte S. Baker, should add to releasing your doubts and fears when you come to God in prayer. The words of the refrain are:

Why should I worry why should I fear,
When the very same Jesus He stays always near,
He lives in my heart and He hears when I cry,
I'll call on the master till the storm passes by.

Once one becomes cultural-oriented, it is difficult to transition into becoming one who is enraptured. Enculturation is another word for socialization. It conveys the idea that it is: "The process whereby individuals learn their group's culture, through experience, observation, and instruction." Enraptured conveys the meaning of one who is: "delighted beyond measure." It is one who is filled with: "ecstatic joy or delight; joyful ecstasy." When this is applied to how and why one gathers with others to worship, the question is if one is doing so to feel fulfilled by a particular form and ritual or by being engaged in a personal relationship with the Triune God? In John 4, there is a classic example regarding form and ritual versus personal engagement in worship. On His journey with the disciples, an interesting statement is made in John 4:4 (NASB), "And He had to pass through Samaria." Actually, He chose to go through Samaria because He had something specific He wanted to accomplish. After a personal interaction with the woman at the well, we read about His specific purpose in John 4:21-26 (ESV), where Jesus converses with the woman at the well.

> Jesus said to her, Woman, believe me, the hour is coming when neither on this mountain nor in Jerusalem will you worship the Father. You worship what you do not know; we worship what we know, for salvation is from the Jews. But the hour is coming, and is now here, when the true worshipers will worship the Father in spirit and truth, for the Father is seeking such people to worship Him. God is spirit, and those who worship Him must worship in spirit and truth. The woman said to Him, I know that Messiah is coming (he who is called Christ). When He comes, He will tell us all things. Jesus said to her, I who speak to you am He.

Jesus is emphasizing the time and place when personal and purposeful relationship to the Triune God will far outweigh all form and ritual. God is not found in the form but He is found in a personal relationship through the Lord Jesus Christ.

A transition will occur in regard to focus on mission and purpose. It is at this point, we read (verses 27-30): "His disciples came, and they were amazed that He had been speaking with a woman, yet no one said, What do You seek? Why do You speak with her? So the woman left her water-pot, and went into the city and said to the men, Come, see a man who told me all the things that I have done; this is not the Christ, is it? They went out of the city, and were coming to Him." In this sense, the woman was unafraid to witness to others about the Christ she had just met by the well. The disciples are focused on the food they had purchased and failed to notice the woman returning with a group of men. We see Jesus using all of this as an instructional moment for His disciples in terms of priorities they should have in ministry. The text indicates (verses 31-36):

> Meanwhile the disciples were urging Him, saying, Rabbi, eat. But He said to them, I have food to eat that you do not know about. So the disciples were saying to one another, No one brought Him anything to eat, did he? Jesus said to them, My food is to do the will of Him who sent Me and to accomplish His work. Do you not say, there are yet four months, and then comes the harvest? Behold, I say to you, lift up your eyes and look on the fields, that they are white for harvest. Already he who reaps is receiving wages and is gathering fruit for life eternal; so that he who sows and he who reaps may rejoice together.

At this point, Jesus may have directed their attention in the direction where the woman had gone. She is now returning with a group of people to meet with the one who told her, "I Am the Messiah - the one who should be the object of both your spiritual relationship and worship."

The focus, commitment and occasion to worship should always be The Person of Jesus Christ and not The Place that a group of people have designated where such worship should take place. Worship is always spiritual in nature versus physical in terms of location. The force of Hebrews 11 embodies the idea of being enraptured as one worships the Living God and Savior. Hebrews 11:1-2, 6 (ESV) shares with us:

> Now faith is the assurance of things hoped for, the conviction of things not seen. For by it the people of old received their commendation. By faith Enoch was taken up...Now before he was taken he was commended as having pleased God. And without faith it is impossible to please him, for whoever would draw near to God must believe that he exists and that he rewards those who seek him.

THE TWENTY-FIRST CENTURY CHURCH: IS IT WAXING OR WANING

The phrase that should be noticed and remembered is that our objective in Christian faith and practice is that we are to "please Him" in all that we do or say. Anything short of that is ritual and form. As we draw a distinction between being cultural-oriented versus being enraptured, words from a hymn, "Face To Face" written by Carrie E. Breck (1898) share the intent of what it means for one to be enraptured in a personal commitment and infatuation with Jesus Christ alone. The first stanza and refrain convey the thought:

Face to face with Christ, my Savior,
Face to face—what will it be,
When with rapture I behold Him,
Jesus Christ who died for me?

Refrain

Face to face I shall behold Him,
Far beyond the starry sky;
Face to face in all His glory,
I shall see Him by and by!

Does Jesus Christ have the preeminent place in your life? Is He the center of your daily walk and the decisions you make? Is your spiritual life one that is waxing or waning? If you are growing in the grace and knowledge of the Lord Jesus Christ, then you are waxing! If not, then you are waning! May you always desire to live your life in the joy and with the strength of the Lord.

12. Constructing Crafty Narratives

So Jesus was saying to those Jews who had believed Him, If you continue in My word, then you are truly disciples of Mine; and you will know the truth, and the truth will make you free.
John 8:31-32 (NASB)

Jesus said: I am the way, and the truth, and the life; no one comes to the Father but through Me.
John 14:6

     In a day of cultural demise, is the invisible Church of the Lord Jesus Christ a visible and viable presence in the world? How is the Gospel being validated in our day? What religion does the secular society speak of more than any other? Why has the Church of Jesus Christ allowed itself to become marginalized by the culture? Has the message of the Church become compromised by societal niceties and desire for community acceptance? When the culture begins to gain influence, it usually impacts major areas of life. In recent years, we have witnessed this influence in politics, education, international affairs, moral standards and the Church. The areas affected at the outset are foundational principles, scruples ("a moral or ethical consideration or standard that acts as a restraining force or inhibits certain actions" (*dictionary.com*) and integrity. In the year 2015, we appear to have reached a zenith (a highest point or state; culmination) in terms of evil and wickedness that is dominating the culture of the entire world. Deceit and deception join together and become paramount ("chief in importance or impact") within the governance of the various institutions that define what a nation is and who the people of the nation desire to be. Apathy and indifference have become a cancer within nations and the Church is more concerned for its self-preservation rather than being front and center in facing the immediacy of the challenges facing humanity in the twenty-first century. What can be done and what should the Biblical Christian be doing?

In the United States of America, the constitution became the guiding set of foundational principles by which the people of the land would be governed. The Preamble indicates:

> We the People of the United States, in Order to form a more perfect Union, establish Justice, insure domestic Tranquility, provide for the common defense, promote the general Welfare, and secure the Blessings of Liberty to ourselves and our Posterity, do ordain and establish this Constitution for the United States of America.

Whether or not the nation now fully appreciates Constitutional Government is being tested. In the balance, truth and justice both for this nation and in the world, is teetering. We witness this when an election to a particular political office nears and a tool that is frequently used is the creation of a narrative about one's opponent. Many times the narrative that has been constructed is either misleading or a complete falsehood. The idea behind the use of the crafty narrative is to create doubt in the mind of the voter. A classic example of this is the news that has surfaced in March 2015 about the presidential election campaigns in 2012. The Senate Majority Leader, Harry Reid (Democrat, Nevada) made blatantly false statements about presidential candidate, Mitt Romney. On September 25, 2012, Fox News Politics reported, "Senate Majority Leader Harry Reid lashed out at Mitt Romney's faith during a conference call with reporters, saying he is not the face of Mormonism and suggesting he has tarnished the religion. Reid, a Democrat and the highest-ranking Mormon in U. S. elected office, also said he agrees with claims that Romney has sullied the Latter-day Saints faith." In another statement, in *The Washington Post*, July 31, 2012, "Senate Majority Leader Harry Reid (D-Nev.) claimed…in an interview that Republican presidential candidate Mitt Romney refuses to release additional tax returns because he didn't pay taxes for 10 years. The interview, published in *The Huffington Post*, includes several swipes by the Senate leader at the GOP candidate." More recently, newsbusters.org posted a portion of an interview with Senator Harry Reid, where the following exchanges occurred on *CNN's* New Day -March 31, 2015:

> DANA BASH: You're a polarizing figure, and a lot of Republicans actually blame you personally for the way Congress and Washington in general has gotten so highly partisan in the past couple of years.
>
> HARRY REID: That's interesting. I served as the whip for a long time, and the Republicans were effusive in their praise for me.
>
> BASH: That was before he used the Senate Floor to go after GOP mega-donors the Koch brothers and accused Mitt Romney of not paying his taxes with no evidence.
> (From A VIDEOTAPE OF REID ON SENATE FLOOR: Let him prove he's paid taxes. Because he hasn't.)
>
> REID (returning to current interview): No, I don't regret that at all. The Koch brothers. No one would help me, they were afraid they'd go after them. So I did it on my own. That's what I felt I had to do.
>
> BASH: So no regrets about Mitt Romney, the Koch Brothers? Some people have even called it "McCarthyite."
>
> REID: Well, they can call it whatever they want. Romney didn't win, did he?

The narrative was constructed to diminish an opponent's religious scruples and his financial integrity and all of it deemed justifiable with the rationale, "Romney didn't win, did he?" Credence is given to the notion that it is all right to lie, mislead, misrepresent, falsify and malign an individual because the end justifies the means whereas foundational principles, moral values, personal integrity and the maintenance of that which is honorable can all be sacrificed because winning at any cost and by any means is what governs the body politic. What a travesty and legacy this leaves as an example for generations to come.

A second example of the use of that which is misleading or a falsehood is in the area of racial considerations in the nation. One example of this is the recent riots in Ferguson, Missouri following the police shooting of Michael Brown. His death was an occasion for racist advocates to propound a constructed narrative that was known to be misleading and false. On August 8, 2014 *The Washington Post* reported the following based upon the Department of Justice findings:

> (The Police Officer) Wilson knew about the theft of the cigarillos from the convenience store and had a description of the suspects. (Michael) Brown fought with the officer and tried to take his gun. And the popular hands-up storyline, which isn't corroborated by ballistic and DNA evidence and multiple witness statements, was perpetuated by Witness 101. In fact, just about everything said to the media by Witness 101, whom we all know as Dorian Johnson, the friend with Brown that day, was not supported by the evidence and other witness statements.
>
> Fight in the SUV - Page 6: Wilson and other witnesses stated that Brown then reached into the SUV through the open driver's window and punched and grabbed Wilson. This is corroborated by bruising on Wilson's jaw and scratches on his neck, the presence of Brown's DNA on Wilson's collar, shirt, and pants, and

Wilson's DNA on Brown's palm. While there are other individuals who stated that Wilson reached out of the SUV and grabbed Brown by the neck, prosecutors could not credit their accounts because they were inconsistent with physical and forensic evidence, as detailed throughout this report.

Struggle over the gun - Page 6: Brown then grabbed the weapon and struggled with Wilson to gain control of it. Wilson fired, striking Brown in the hand. Autopsy results and bullet trajectory, skin from Brown's palm on the outside of the SUV door as well as Brown's DNA on the inside of the driver's door corroborate Wilson's account that during the struggle, Brown used his right hand to grab and attempt to control Wilson's gun. According to three autopsies, Brown sustained a close range gunshot wound to the fleshy portion of his right hand at the base of his right thumb. Soot from the muzzle of the gun found embedded in the tissue of this wound coupled with indicia of thermal change from the heat of the muzzle indicate that Brown's hand was within inches of the muzzle of Wilson's gun when it was fired. The location of the recovered bullet in the side panel of the driver's door, just above Wilson's lap, also corroborates Wilson's account of the struggle over the gun and when the gun was fired, as do witness accounts that Wilson fired at least one shot from inside the SUV.

Hands up - Page 8: Although there are several individuals who have stated that Brown held his hands up in an unambiguous sign of surrender prior to Wilson shooting him dead, their accounts do not support a prosecution of Wilson. As detailed throughout this report, some of those accounts are inaccurate because they are inconsistent with the physical and forensic evidence; some of those accounts are materially inconsistent with that witness's own prior statements with no explanation, credible [or] otherwise, as to why those accounts changed over time. Certain other witnesses who originally stated Brown had his hands up in surrender recanted their original accounts, admitting that they did not witness the shooting or parts of it, despite what they initially reported either to federal or local law enforcement or to the media. Prosecutors did not rely on those accounts when making a prosecutive decision.

While credible witnesses gave varying accounts of exactly what Brown was doing with his hands as he moved toward Wilson – i.e., balling them, holding them out, or pulling up his pants up – and varying accounts of how he was moving – i.e., "charging," moving in "slow motion," or "running" – they all establish that Brown was moving toward Wilson when Wilson shot him. Although some witnesses state that Brown held his hands up at shoulder level with his palms facing outward for a brief moment, these same witnesses describe Brown then dropping his hands and "charging" at Wilson.

The DOJ report notes on page 44 that Johnson "made multiple statements to the media immediately following the incident that spawned the popular narrative that Wilson shot Brown execution-style as he held up his hands in surrender." In one of those interviews, Johnson told MSNBC that Brown was shot in the back by Wilson. It was then that Johnson said Brown stopped, turned around with his hands up and said, "I don't have a gun, stop shooting!" And, like that, "hands up, don't shoot" became the mantra of a movement. But it was wrong, built on a lie.

Racial Advocates perpetuated that which the Department of Justice indicated. "Hands up, Don't Shoot" became the mantra of a movement. But it was wrong, built on a lie! Along came a bombastic individual to promote the misleading and false narrative, Alfred Charles (Al) Sharpton Jr., is an American Baptist minister and civil rights activist. According to Wikipedia, "Sharpton's supporters praise his ability and willingness to defy the power structure that is seen as the cause of their suffering and consider him a man who is willing to tell it like it is." One would hope that his guiding principles would be integrity, accuracy, the maintenance of calm and peace. One of the many qualifications for one who bears the title, "Reverend," is that he must be a man who adheres to the principle: "So then we pursue the things which make for peace and the building up of one another" (Romans 14:19). This same idea is echoed in Hebrews 12:14, "Make every effort to live in peace with everyone." If only Mr. Sharpton would learn and implement the principles in the prayer of St. Francis of Assisi, "Lord, make me an instrument of your peace, Where there is hatred, let me sow love; where there is injury, pardon; where there is doubt, faith; where there is despair, hope; where there is darkness, light; where there is sadness, joy…" This implementation could have a positive impact and offer words of wisdom for those who feel trapped and ensnared in the self-perpetuating racial quagmire.

The third illustration pertains to a treaty agreement between several nations who wish to stipulate what Iran is permitted to do with nuclear development and proliferation. The President of the United States, Barrack Obama and the Secretary of State, John Kerry represented to the American people that they had tacit agreement by Iran to certain principles and conditions regarding nuclear development. The United States Senate was being asked to not get involved in the treaty negotiations by passing a bill that would increase the number of sanctions upon Iran. Meanwhile, *CNS News Service* (CNSnews.com) reported on April 10, 2015 the following:

Iranian supreme leader Ayatollah Ali Khamenei delivers a major speech on Thursday, April 9, 2015.

(CNSNews.com) – In his keenly-awaited reaction to the provisional nuclear deal announced in Switzerland a week ago, Iranian supreme leader Ayatollah Ali Khamenei on Thursday attacked a key pillar of the entire deal being promoted by the Obama administration – the question of inspections of suspect sites in Iran.

The administration has characterized the International Atomic Energy Agency (IAEA) inspection regime to be put in place under a final Iran agreement as the most intrusive and comprehensive ever devised.

Not only must Iran allow IAEA inspectors to "have regular access to all of Iran's [declared] nuclear facilities," according to an official U.S. fact sheet of "parameters" of the framework agreement, it must moreover "grant access to the IAEA to investigate suspicious sites or allegations of a covert enrichment facility, conversion facility, centrifuge production facility, or yellowcake production facility anywhere in the country."

But that Iran agreed to such a provision – admitting inspectors on demand to any suspicious site anywhere in the country – is now under dispute. In his speech Khamenei called the fact sheet an example of White House "lying".

Khamenei also challenged other points in the U.S. version of what had been agreed to at the talks in Lausanne, including the timing of the lifting of sanctions – both those measures imposed under U.N. Security Council resolutions as well as U.S. and European Union nuclear-related sanctions.

The administration's parameters document ties sanctions relief to Iran verifiably abiding to its commitments. But the supreme leader demanded that they be lifted immediately the final deal is signed.

THE TWENTY-FIRST CENTURY CHURCH: IS IT WAXING OR WANING

> Instant annulment of all sanctions is one of the demands of our officials, he said. This issue is very important, and the sanctions must all be completely removed on the day of the agreement.

In different commentary and punditry, another narrative begins to unfold. It is suggested that the administration is incompetent, gullible or naive. The suggestion is that micro-management without consultation with the full Congress and military leadership demonstrates weakness and a lack of governmental authority. The strategy is deemed to be leading from behind. This causes other nations to doubt American resolve and trustworthiness. The allies are hesitant to have confidence in America and the enemies see no reason to have any fear or respect for the President and the nation.

Does this mean that the United States of America is in a state of irreversible decline? When I was a young lad, prophetic teachers were prominent with the predictions about world events and the alignment of nations. The question was asked: "Why is there no indication of the United States of America in biblical prophecy?" Other prominent nations spoken of in newscasts can be identified, but not the USA. I remember one of the speculations was that America would be so closely aligned with Israel so that whatever was said about or to Israel would be a reference to America as well. Another speculation following World War II was that America would be so decimated by a military attack (atomic or nuclear) that the nation would become insignificant and incapable of having any meaningful involvement in world matters and affairs.

A word from The Word corroborates the possibility of a nation's potential but also its demise. The basic idea of God for His people is given in Deuteronomy 28:1-2.

> And if you faithfully obey the voice of the Lord your God, being careful to do all his commandments that I

command you today, the Lord your God will set you high above all the nations of the earth. And all these blessings shall come upon you and overtake you, if you obey the voice of the Lord your God.

We need to ask the question concerning the direction of the United States of America, "Is the nation bent on doing God's will and way or has it prescribed something of its own design?" A problem that develops is that a nation can begin to construct a crafty narrative about what it wants to be and how it wants to be known. If it does so with the abandonment of God and His Word, then it has jettisoned the moral compass as well. This nation may well be defined by Proverbs 14:34, "Righteousness exalts a nation, but sin is a reproach to any people." There should be no straddling of this fence. We are either a nation that is committed to righteousness or one that delights in sinful alternatives.

When a nation allows itself to be self-sufficient and frees itself from any need for fear of God, it does so to its own peril. The Prophet Isaiah brought this Word from God to the nations of his day (Isaiah 40:15-18).

> Behold, the nations are like a drop from a bucket, And are regarded as a speck of dust on the scales; Behold, He lifts up the islands like fine dust. Even Lebanon is not enough to burn, Nor its beasts enough for a burnt offering All the nations are as nothing before Him, They are regarded by Him as less than nothing and meaningless. To whom then will you liken God? Or what likeness will you compare with Him?

How do you answer the last two questions posed by Isaiah: "To whom do you liken God and what likeness will you compare with Him?" Before we attempt an answer for these Biblical considerations, we should review an additional thought recorded in Ecclesiastes 5:1-3.

THE TWENTY-FIRST CENTURY CHURCH: IS IT WAXING OR WANING

> Guard your steps as you go to the house of God and draw near to listen rather than to offer the sacrifice of fools; for they do not know they are doing evil. Do not be hasty in word or impulsive in thought to bring up a matter in the presence of God. For God is in heaven and you are on the earth; therefore let your words be few. For the dream comes through much effort and the voice of a fool through many words.

As one approaches God's throne, is there a place for the construction of crafty narratives? Would it be wise to do so? What should one's perspective be about God? How should one approach the omniscient (all-knowing) God?

There is a Scriptural Guideline that represents the standard for truth. It is also an instruction regarding how well interaction between persons can be maximized as each one is committed to the standard of lifestyle and communication. These are not mechanical steps that can be arbitrarily selected and applied. The only way these words can be functional in one's life is by and in a personal relationship with Jesus Christ. These things are spiritual matters that will flow out from one who is embracing God's truth and will as a lifestyle choice. It should be noted that the required spiritual lifestyle must be dominant in one's life. Observe God's word to each of us stated precisely and in an all-encompassing manner.

> Since you have heard about Jesus and have learned the truth that comes from him, throw off your old sinful nature and your former way of life, which is corrupted by lust and deception. Instead, let the Spirit renew your thoughts and attitudes. Put on your new nature, created to be like God—truly righteous and holy. So stop telling lies. Let us tell our neighbors the truth, for we are all parts of the same body. And don't sin by letting anger control you. Don't let the sun go down while you are still

angry, for anger gives a foothold to the devil. If you are a thief, quit stealing. Instead, use your hands for good hard work, and then give generously to others in need. Don't use foul or abusive language. Let everything you say be good and helpful, so that your words will be an encouragement to those who hear them. And do not bring sorrow to God's Holy Spirit by the way you live. Remember, he has identified you as his own, guaranteeing that you will be saved on the day of redemption. Get rid of all bitterness, rage, anger, harsh words, and slander, as well as all types of evil behavior. Instead, be kind to each other, tenderhearted, forgiving one another, just as God through Christ has forgiven you. (Ephesians 4:21-31, NLT)

We have no way to prove or demonstrate that a secular world any longer is watching the visible Church. Once the Church allowed itself to adapt to some cultural ways and values, there was no longer a clear light emanating from the Church and piercing the darkness. The adapting to or condoning of cultural values has contributed to the Church's waning and declining whereas it should be waxing and thriving. It's not too late to amend our ways and put aside our crafted narratives, rituals and formalities. We must desire and seek the work of Jesus Christ in us and through us. The world needs to hear the non-compromised and unvarnished message of the Word of God. May we be part of that message and that mission for the Lord Jesus Christ!

13. Analysis and Determination

> *Enter through the narrow gate; for the gate is wide and the way is broad that leads to destruction, and there are many who enter through it. For the gate is small and the way is narrow that leads to life, and there are few who find it. Beware of the false prophets, who come to you in sheep's clothing, but inwardly are ravenous wolves. You will know them by their fruits. Not everyone who says to Me, Lord, Lord, will enter the kingdom of heaven, but he who does the will of My Father who is in heaven. Many will say to Me on that day, Lord, Lord, did we not prophesy in Your name, and in Your name cast out demons, and in Your name perform many miracles? And then I will declare to them, I never knew you; Depart from Me you who practice lawlessness.*
> Matthew 7:13-23 (Selected - NASB)

How should the Church and biblical Christian approach the deterioration of sound values and principles in the culture and visible Church? It cannot be stressed too often that accommodation or adaptation to the desires of the Culture is not the acceptable alternative for the 21st Century Church. Those who have attempted to do so have become a part of the problem rather than contributing toward a solution in any purposeful way. The trends at the present time is summarized in a *Christian Post* article dated, April 11, 2015 by Larry Tomczak and titled, "Could Nationwide Gay Nuptials Be Judgment for Cowardly Church Leadership?" Part of what he posted in his article was the following:

> Masses are being led to accept that every man can do what is right in his own eyes (Judges 21:25). No one should judge or discriminate if someone loves another person or persons. The ultimate goal is not merely legalized Gay "marriage" but total sexual freedom

including all of the following: Homosexuality and gay marriage; Bisexuality; Transsexuality; Pederasty (Gay relationship between adult and adolescent); Promiscuity; Polygamy; Polyamory (multiple partners); Cohabitation (fornication); Open marriages (adultery); Pornography

Not all of the above are checked off their to do list (yet). They are working aggressively and are well financed and organized to achieve their goals. The above constitutes sexual anarchy. Barring divine intervention through a heaven-sent awakening, this is the slippery slope upon which America finds itself today. The reason Christians are targeted and intimidated is because we represent the last obstacle in their quest for unrestrained sexual licentiousness.

The commission of the Lord Jesus Christ to His Church should be paramount in the Biblical Christian's thinking and mindset. One's compassion toward the Culture must never become confused with complicity in the behavior patterns of the culture. One's conversation should never become condescending or condoning in any way. God's standards should never be relegated to being compromised with the cultural demands. The choice should be clearcut - God's Commands and not Mankind's Demands. The requirement and task for a disciple of the Lord Jesus Christ has never varied or been modified. Minimally, Luke 9:23-26 is instruction by Jesus and what He expects from His followers.

> Jesus was saying to them all: If anyone wishes to come after Me, he must deny himself, and take up his cross daily and follow Me. For whoever wishes to save his life will lose it, but whoever loses his life for My sake, he is the one who will save it. For what is a man profited if he gains the whole world, and loses or forfeits himself? For whoever is ashamed of Me and My words, the Son of

THE TWENTY-FIRST CENTURY CHURCH: IS IT WAXING OR WANING

> Man will be ashamed of him when He comes in His glory, and the glory of the Father and of the holy angels.

It is obvious that the expectation of Jesus is threefold. First is to understand and be committed to denying oneself the pleasures and pleasantries that non-followers desire and enjoy. Second is to be identified with the cross by being identified with it daily, that is, maintaining a 24/7 identity and relationship with Jesus Christ. Third is to be a consistent follower of Jesus Christ. Disciples who are committed to Jesus Christ should know there will be challenges and hardships as one engages the culture and the backslidden Churches. The task is formidable and the path will not be one that will allow the making of many friends or being readily accepted or sought.

When Paul wrote the Pastoral Epistles to Timothy and Titus, he highlighted at least five significant emphases for ministry objectives. Depending upon the Bible translation one uses, the reference will be to "the faithful" (KJV) or "the trustworthy" (ESV, NASB) statements. The Greek construction of the phrase is πιστος ο λογος, literally "faith the word" or simply "The Word (of) Faith." This is the phrase used in the five citations in the Pastoral Epistles. In considering these five points of emphasis, one can become reminded and refocused on the true objectives and requirements of being a good servant of the Lord Jesus Christ. It should also be noted and understood that all Scripture is inspired by God and is faithful and true. The following words to Timothy and Titus are intended to demonstrate and challenge them to accept and implement the truths that Paul is emphasizing when he uses the phrasing, "faithful saying" or "trustworthy statement. "The first occurrence of the phrase appears in I Timothy 1:15-16.

> It is a trustworthy statement, deserving full acceptance, that Christ Jesus came into the world to save sinners, among whom I am foremost of all. Yet for this reason I

found mercy, so that in me as the foremost, Jesus Christ might demonstrate His perfect patience as an example for those who would believe in Him for eternal life.

The thrust of the text pertains to and emphasizes why Jesus Christ came into the world. It was to save sinners. During the earthly ministry of Jesus Christ, all kinds of people were coming to either dine with Him or to be instructed by Him. On one occasion, His sole mission and purpose is clearly stated in Matthew 9:10-13 (ESV).

And as Jesus reclined at table in the house, behold, many tax collectors and sinners came and were reclining with Jesus and his disciples. And when the Pharisees saw this, they said to his disciples, Why does your teacher eat with tax collectors and sinners? But when he heard it, he said, Those who are well have no need of a physician, but those who are sick. Go and learn what this means, I desire mercy, and not sacrifice. For I came not to call the righteous, but sinners.

When Paul contemplated these words of Jesus, he took that in the most personal way and he applied it to himself as well as in his ministry. The words are clear, "So that in me...Jesus Christ might demonstrate His perfect patience as an example for those who would believe in Him for eternal life." The Gospel is clear and the responsibility to convey it precisely is equally clear.

The second occurrence is I Timothy 3:1 (NASB). "It is a trustworthy statement (faithful saying): if any man aspires to the office of overseer, it is a fine work he desires to do."

In *Baker's Evangelical Dictionary of Biblical Theology*, there is extensive discussion about the meaning of the overseer. Part of that discussion states:

The word overseer (Greek: *episkopos*) is used a limited number of times in the New Testament, but it has significant implications for a proper understanding of leadership in the Church. The noun *episkopos* appears five times in the New Testament and means overseer, guardian, bishop. It is used in reference to Jesus Christ in 1 Peter 2:25 and in other places of individuals who have a function of leadership in the Church (Acts 20:28 ; Philippians 1:1 ; 1 Timothy 3:2 ; Titus 1:7). The verb *episkopeo* appears in 1 Peter 5:2 and means to take care of, to oversee, or to care for. It appears in 1 Timothy 3:1 and refers to the position or office of overseer or bishop. It seems clear that a plurality of overseers (elders) was the New Testament model, though flexibility apparently existed as to structure. It is quite likely that one overseer or elder would have primary leadership as the pastor among the other elders in the local Church, such as James in the Church at Jerusalem (cf. Acts 15:13-21). The office itself is restricted to men. As men are called to be the spiritual leaders in the home, so they are to be the spiritual leaders in the Church (1 Corinthians 11:2-16; Ephesians 5:21-33; 1 Timothy 2:9-3:7).

The third occurrence pertains to the good servant's personal disciplines is stated in I Timothy 4:7-9.

> In pointing out these things to the brethren, you will be a good servant of Christ Jesus, constantly nourished on the words of the faith and of the sound doctrine which you have been following. But have nothing to do with worldly fables fit only for old women. On the other hand, discipline yourself for the purpose of godliness; for bodily discipline is only of little profit, but godliness is profitable for all things, since it holds promise for the present life and also for the life to come. It is a trustworthy (faithful) statement deserving full acceptance. For it is for this we labor and strive, because

we have fixed our hope on the living God, who is the Savior of all men, especially of believers." The focus is on "discipline yourself for the purpose of godliness.

The servant of the Lord is to pursue holiness, righteousness, sanctification and godliness. In II Peter 1:2-3, Peter shared: "Grace and peace be multiplied to you in the knowledge of God and of Jesus our Lord; seeing that His divine power has granted to us everything pertaining to life and godliness, through the true knowledge of Him who called us by His own glory and excellence." The emphasis is in desiring to be like Jesus Christ and disciplining oneself in all areas of life so that goal can and will be achieved. One's life should be lived according to the words of an old camp chorus written by Alfred B. Smith in 1941.

> *With eternity's values in view, Lord.*
> *With eternity's values in view;*
> *May I do each day's work for Jesus*
> *With eternity's values in view.*

It is based upon the words of Scripture in I John 3:2, "Beloved, now we are children of God, and it has not appeared as yet what we will be. We know that when He appears, we will be like Him, because we will see Him just as He is. And everyone who has this hope fixed on Him purifies himself, just as He is pure."

The fourth occurrence is II Timothy 2:11-13.

> It is a trustworthy (faithful) statement: For if we died with Him, we will also live with Him; If we endure, we will also reign with Him; If we deny Him, He also will deny us; If we are faithless, He remains faithful, for He cannot deny Himself.

THE TWENTY-FIRST CENTURY CHURCH: IS IT WAXING OR WANING

Paul is indicating a uniqueness in identification with Jesus Christ. The idea is that believers are seen by God as identified with Christ in his death, so we also shall go to live with Christ in heaven, to be forever with Him. Elsewhere, Paul has stated his personal commitment and desire.

> I count all things to be loss in view of the surpassing value of knowing Christ Jesus my Lord, for whom I have suffered the loss of all things, and count them but rubbish so that I may gain Christ, and may be found in Him, not having a righteousness of my own derived from the Law, but that which is through faith in Christ, the righteousness which comes from God on the basis of faith, that I may know Him and the power of His resurrection and the fellowship of His sufferings, being conformed to His death; in order that I may attain to the resurrection from the dead. (Philippians 3:8-11)

In another passage, Galatians 2:20 Paul stated: "I have been crucified with Christ; and it is no longer I who live, but Christ lives in me; and the life which I now live in the flesh I live by faith in the Son of God, who loved me and gave Himself up for me." I am fond of the words written by Oswald J. Smith in 1914:

> *Into the heart of Jesus Deeper and deeper I go,*
> *Seeking to know the reason Why He should love me so,*
> *Why He should stoop to lift me Up from the miry clay,*
> *Saving my soul, making me whole,*
> *Though I had wandered away.*

> *Into the will of Jesus, Deeper and deeper I go,*
> *Praying for grace to follow, Seeking His way to know;*
> *Bowing in full surrender Low at His blessed feet,*
> *Bidding Him take, break me and make,*
> *Till I am molded, complete.*

James Perry

Into the love of Jesus Deeper and deeper I go,
Praising the One who brought me Out of my sin and woe;
And through eternal ages Gratefully I shall sing,
O how He loved! O how He loved!
Jesus, my Lord and my king!

The fifth occurrence of faithful and trustworthy statement is Titus 3:5-10.

> He saved us, not on the basis of deeds which we have done in righteousness, but according to His mercy, by the washing of regeneration and renewing by the Holy Spirit, whom He poured out upon us richly through Jesus Christ our Savior, so that being justified by His grace we would be made heirs according to the hope of eternal life. This is a trustworthy statement; and concerning these things I want you to speak confidently, so that those who have believed God will be careful to engage in good deeds. These things are good and profitable for men. But avoid foolish controversies and genealogies and strife and disputes about the Law, for they are unprofitable and worthless. Reject a factious man after a first and second warning, knowing that such a man is perverted and is sinning, being self-condemned.

The one justified by God's grace is made an heir of eternal life. This reality is not based upon feeling but the faith-fact that God has set forth for His followers. Because of this reality, the Apostle Paul instructs Titus to continually tell the believers in Christ that they should be diligent about doing good works, not just occasionally, but to seek opportunity for doing them, for in so-doing this is good and profitable unto men. He then mentions some unprofitable and vain things that Christian's should avoid and not do. The Christian life is lived on a continuum, not on a tee-ter-totter. The follower of Christ is to be knowledgeable regarding the Christian experience and how to walk triumphantly and confidently upon the firm foundation of God's Word and Authority.

There has to be a careful reading and understanding of Titus 3:5-10. First, "He saved us, not on the basis of deeds which we have done in righteousness." It is consistent with the thrust of Ephesians 2:8-9 (ESV), "For by grace you have been saved through faith. And this is not your own doing; it is the gift of God, not a result of works, so that no one may boast." Salvation is all of God's grace and not by any degree of works of righteousness that any person done. However, there is an important factor that must be acted upon, "Those who have believed God will be careful to engage in good deeds. These things are good and profitable for men." This is also consistent with Ephesians 2:10, "For we are his workmanship, created in Christ Jesus for good works, which God prepared beforehand, that we should walk in them." No one who believes is designed or destined to live out redemption in a vacuum or a sanitized bubble that would allow the person to be isolated from ordinary activities of life or those things that flow from a degenerate, evil and wicked generation. No one can deny the presence and influences of wickedness and evil within the culture. A principle of faith and practice is stated in Romans 5:20-21 (NIV), "But where sin increased, grace increased all the more, so that, just as sin reigned in death, so also grace might reign through righteousness to bring eternal life through Jesus Christ our Lord." There are questions one must answer and decisions one must make. Is the Almighty God limited to when, where and how His Grace can infiltrate any and all cultures that are present in the world? Is sin increasing in the culture and world? Is grace operative at all times and in all cultures? The real issue seems to be one's concept of self-preservation and being well thought of by other people. We need to remember that those who have been redeemed by the riches of God's grace have a duty to represent the Gospel in the world. Paul stated precisely to Titus (3:5-10), "Those who have believed God will be careful to engage in good deeds. These things are good and profitable for men." Those who are redeemed "will be careful to engage in good deeds" that are "good and profitable for men (mankind)."

There are two other usages of the "faithful saying" or "trustworthy" phrases. The first is Revelation 21:5 (NIV), "He who was seated on the throne said, I am making everything new! Then he said, Write this down, for these words are trustworthy and true." **our** focus is the final phrase of the verse, "These words are trustworthy and true." In the Nestle Greek Text, 1904, the phrase is: οτι ουτοι οι λόγοι πιστοσ και άληθινοί εστιν. The meaning is, "These are faith words and true words." They are intended for those who read and hear them to respond affirmatively to them. This phrase construct also appears elsewhere in The Book of Revelation such as in 3:14 and 19:6. In Revelation 21:5, the thrust is on the truth and certainty of a future new heaven and new earth that is assured by the word and promise of God, and ordered to be committed to writing as a permanent record.

The second additional usage is Revelation 22:6 (NIV), "The angel said to me, These words are trustworthy and true. The Lord, the God who inspires the prophets, sent his angel to show his servants the things that must soon take place." Once again, the Greek text contains "οἱ λόγοι πιστο και άληθινοί" faith words and true words. The context of this passage is giving a description of the New Jerusalem (heaven). This description represents faithful and true words revealed from the throne of God. Do you believe these faithful and trustworthy truths? Have you embraced them by implementing them in your personal faith and life walk? Are you joyful as you take up your cross daily and follow Him? Are you waxing or waning in your Christian faith and practice? Has the 21st Century Church impacted your knowledge of God and His will either positively or negatively? How and in what ways? What do you believe your primary response should be at this point in your life? Are you ready and willing to respond affirmatively and immediately to God's calling and purpose for your life?

THE TWENTY-FIRST CENTURY CHURCH: IS IT WAXING OR WANING

> While walking by the Sea of Galilee, He saw two brothers, Simon (who is called Peter) and Andrew his brother, casting a net into the sea, for they were fishermen. And He said to them, Follow Me, and I will make you fishers of men. Immediately they left their nets and followed Him. And going on from there He saw two other brothers, James the son of Zebedee and John his brother, in the boat with Zebedee their father, mending their nets, and He called them. Immediately they left the boat and their father and followed Him. (Matthew 4:18-22, ESV)

In 1852, Cecil F. Alexander wrote a hymn about Jesus calling disciples to follow Him. How do you respond to the call of Jesus? Are you following Him now? Is Jesus pleased with your approach to following Him? Two of the hymn stanzas contain the following words:

> *Jesus calls us from the worship*
> *Of the vain world's golden store,*
> *From each idol that would keep us,*
> *Saying, Christian, love Me more!*
>
> *Jesus calls us! By Thy mercies,*
> *Savior may we hear Thy call,*
> *Give our hearts to Thine obedience,*
> *Serve and love Thee best of all.*

If the words of this hymn are the basis of your personal commitment to Jesus Christ, then you will be numbered with the biblical Christians who are waxing rather than waning. Similarly, if this is the reality and witness of the visible Church you attend, you will be a particular Church that is waxing and not waning. As and when this is occurring, it allows a certainty that you are adhering to the tenets of the invisible Church of the Lord Jesus Christ. He wants these tenets to be viable and radiating from the visible Church that bears His name. May the Lord bless you and keep you as you grow in the grace and knowledge of the Lord Jesus Christ!

14. Fidelity or Falderal

See how great a love the Father has bestowed on us, that we would be called children of God; and such we are. For this reason the world does not know us, because it did not know Him. Beloved, now we are children of God, and it has not appeared as yet what we will be. We know that when He appears, we will be like Him, because we will see Him just as He is. And everyone who has this hope fixed on Him purifies himself, just as He is pure.
I John 3:1-3 (NASB)

       In 1924, Robert Harkness wrote the words and music to a hymn that asks a question throughout each stanza and chorus, "Why Should He Love Me So?" The 21st Century Church appears to be searching for its identity and meaning in a contemporary culture. Is it a necessary search? Isn't the message of the Church to be about a changeless God and a changeless Gospel? Whatever happened to the Church's belief in, acknowledgement of and subscription to Malachi 3:6 (ESV), "For I the LORD do not change" along with "Before the mountains were brought forth, or ever you had formed the earth and the world, from everlasting to everlasting you are God" (Psalm 90:2, ESV)? As the visible Church struggles through the variations and modifications of the Biblical message, there is evidence that the Church has allowed itself to be in a precarious place as it vacillates about the applications of God's standards for a secular culture. In an effort to be accommodating, the Church has assumed a posture of being all things to all people so that by some means more will respond favorably to the Church and its modified message. Growth, in terms of congregational numbers, has replaced spiritual growth and one's advance matters pertaining to the grace and knowledge of the Lord Jesus Christ.

The broader issue and greater concern for the Church to decipher and determine is in terms of which Banner is upon the Church today. Is it the Agape Church (loved by God) or is it the Ichabod Church (without honor/glory has departed)? The origin given for the word Ichabod on *dictionary.com* states:

> When the tidings of the disastrous defeat of the Israelites in the battle against the Philistines near to Mizpeh were carried to Shiloh, the wife of Phinehas was near to be delivered. And when she heard the tidings that the ark of God was taken, and that her father-in-law and her husband were dead, she bowed herself and travailed (1 Samuel 4:19-22). In her great distress she regarded not the women that stood by her, but named the child that was born Ichabod (no glory), saying, The glory is departed from Israel, and with that word on her lips she expired.

In all generations, the Church will be faced with a decision and a choice. Will the Church maintain fidelity or succumb to the falderal of the day? Based upon Matthew 23:23, the *Forerunner Commentary* (bibletools.org) states:

> The Greek word for faith can also be translated fidelity, as it is in Titus 2:10. To understand what the scribes and Pharisees lacked, we need to examine fidelity along with the traditional definition of faith. *Fidelity*, as defined by Webster, is the quality of being faithful, accuracy in details, exactness. The dictionary adds an interesting modern analogy to explain fidelity: The degree to which an electronic device (as a record player, radio or television) accurately reproduces its effect (as sound or picture). We know we are to bring every thought into captivity to the obedience of Christ (II Corinthians 10:5) and to let this mind be in you which was also in Christ Jesus (Philippians 2:5). John tells us to walk just as He

walked (I John 2:6). Peter advises, Christ…[left] us an example, that you should follow His steps (I Peter 2:21). Spiritually, fidelity is to reproduce faithfully and exactly the thoughts, attitudes, steps, and paths of Jesus Christ. The sounds our lives make on earth reach heaven either as the scratchy, tinny, garbled clanging of carnality and falderal, or as harmonic, melodious, pleasant reproductions of Christ in us, the hope of glory.

The picture one has of falderal within the visible Church is illustrated by an article in the *New York Times* (April 8, 2015) with the Headline: "Biblical Christianity Is What's Stopping Full Acceptance Of The LGBT Agenda." It contains this paragraph:

> The liberal rallying cry these days is that the bible is nothing more than ancient texts with little to meaning or relevance to our daily lives in our cutting edge, technology-laden, social society of 2015…is also prevalent in the worship-du-jour Emergent Church as well. But before you throw out the baby with the bath water, they are right about one thing. The only reason why there has not been an across the board buy-in on the same-sex lifestyle is because the last remnants of biblical Christianity is preventing it. But like the legendary Titanic after it hit the iceberg began to take on water, the professing Christian Church in America has already begun its lisping descent into Laodicean apostasy.

There is a statement written by Frank Bruni in the Op-Ed section of the *New York Times* on April 8, 2015 in which he states:

> Several prominent denominations, which have come to a new understanding of what the Bible does and doesn't decree, of what people can and cannot divine in regard

to God's will. And homosexuality and Christianity don't have to be in conflict in any Church anywhere. That many Christians regard them as incompatible is understandable, an example not so much of hatred's pull as of tradition's sway. Beliefs ossified over centuries aren't easily shaken." A comment made in response to Bruni is: "That's an amazing statement. The Bible very clearly states, in both Testaments, that God is 100% opposed to the same-sex lifestyle, in whatever form it takes. Jesus Himself, in stating that He came to fulfill the Law of Moses which condemns the same-sex lifestyle, also is set against it. The Bible lists as the reason for the collapse of the Church in the last days not from an outward attack, but from an inward collapse. It's called the great Falling Away: Let no man deceive you by any means: for that day shall not come, except there come a falling away first, and that man of sin be revealed, the son of perdition. (II Thessalonians 2:3, KJV)

The Biblical Christian must make a choice regarding fidelity versus the falderal that is penetrating the visible Church. That will mean an unequivocal belief in and commitment to the Word of God as being the only infallible rule of both faith and practice. Those who make allowances for alternative interpretations and lifestyles have departed from the fidelity foundation and shifted to a compromising and accommodating posture with those proposing a secular alternative to the spiritual requirement. In doing so, there is a subscription to that which amounts to falderal (mere nonsense, foolish talk or ideas; trifles). I posted a Blog titled, "Falderal" (April 7, 2015). It may be read in its entirety at: *http://pacafour.blogspot.com*. It contained the following:

> In other words, it all depends subjectively on the one who spends little time in regular reading and studying to determine that which is real and true versus

that which imagined and false. Proverbs 17:27-28 (KJV) shares this word of wisdom and guidance for one's understanding: "He that has knowledge spares his words: and a man of understanding is of an excellent spirit. Even a fool, when he holds his peace, is counted wise: and he that shuts his lips is esteemed as a man of understanding." The NLT renders these verses: "A truly wise person uses few words; a person with understanding is even-tempered. Even fools are thought wise when they keep silent; with their mouths shut, they seem intelligent." A similar thought is shared in Ecclesiastes 5:2, "Do not be hasty in word or impulsive in thought to bring up a matter in the presence of God. For God is in heaven and you are on the earth; therefore let your words be few."

There is another valuable principle regarding one's use of words. It is given in James 1:19-20 (NASB), "But everyone must be quick to hear, slow to speak and slow to anger; for the anger of man does not achieve the righteousness of God. One of the most difficult lessons one has to learn, especially those who are part of the collective clergy, is to be known as one who is quick to hear and slow to speak (or respond)." James has offered good counsel in his epistle in terms of words used and the accompanying falderal, emptiness and meaningless. For instance, in James 2:14-15, "What use is it, my brethren, if someone says he has faith but he has no works? Can that faith save him? If a brother or sister is without clothing and in need of daily food, and one of you says to them, Go in peace, be warmed and be filled, and yet you do not give them what is necessary for their body, what use is that?" Another illustration is given in James 3:5-10, "So also the tongue is a small part of the body, and yet it boasts of great things…And the tongue is a fire, the very world of iniquity; the tongue is set among our members as that which defiles the entire body, and sets on fire the course of our life, and is set on fire by hell…But no one can tame the tongue; it is a restless evil and full of deadly poison. With it we bless our Lord and Father, and with it we curse men, who have been made in the likeness of God; from the same mouth come both blessing and cursing. My brethren, these things ought not to be this way." James is addressing the hypocrisy of one's words and how often a person is complicit in that which is considered to be falderal (mere nonsense, foolish talk or ideas; trifles).

When the Church in any century or time frame begins to condone that which God had condemned, it will no longer be waxing (to increase in extent, quantity, intensity, power) but will rapidly become one that is waning (to decline in power, importance, significance, prosperity and draw to a close as it approaches its end).

Much depends on how the visible Church is established, nurtured and committed to that which is honoring to Jesus Christ. When it becomes an establishment of man's design and structure, it will fail. If it is desirous to be conformed to God's purpose and mission for the particular members of the visible Church, it should be on the path for effective and fruitful ministry for Jesus Christ and His kingdom. There needs to be a clear understanding of Scripture when one reads a passage, such as Matthew 16:15-19 (NLT), Jesus is speaking: "Now I say to you that you are Peter (which means rock), and upon this rock I will build My Church, and all the powers of hell will not conquer it." Jesus clearly defines the foundation and values for His Church that He is building through and by His faithful servants. His words are like a clarion call: "I will build My Church, and all the powers of hell will not conquer it." When Jesus references "My Church," He is speaking about His Bride, the Invisible Church.

THE TWENTY-FIRST CENTURY CHURCH: IS IT WAXING OR WANING

The word Church (often used to define *ecclesia*) contains the meaning of it being a place where people gather. When I was a boy, my family went to a Sunday School where people met in a place called the Gospel Meeting House. It was a long hall with a platform at the front. The seats were moveable and every other connected row of seats was turned around to form a place where the various Sunday School Classes would meet. It was a very practical *ecclesia* where people met for worship and study. It was a model of the term ecclesia which means a place where people were summoned to assemble. It would refer to a congregation gathering to be part of a worship service but it could also be a political forum where people are invited to hear some issue raised or debated. Where a group of people gather together to worship and hear the Word of God is of little significance. Why a group of people meet is far more important than where they meet. When meeting as a Church entity, what is the purpose of the meeting? Is it to worship the Holy and Living God, or is it just a time to visit with one another?

The Book of Acts references the Church beginning and meeting in various homes. The Book of Hebrews (Chapter 11) speaks of people of faith huddled in the dens and caves of the earth. An article in *http://yellowhammernews.com/Faithandculture/how-a-secret-Church-meeting-in-alabama-became-a-worldwide-phenomenon/* (April 2015) gives a report about the Secret Church meeting in various places in Asia for the past few years. Despite the hardships and inconveniences, the movement has realized growth and commitment by the people. They meet in secret places because of the closed society structure of a country. Christianity is unacceptable and will not be tolerated. Socialism, Communism and Islam are opposed to Christians, the Bible, Jesus Christ and The Gospel. One of the atrocities of the ISIS (Islamic State In Syria, now spread into Iraq, Yemen, Libya and elsewhere) movement in the Middle East is not only their attack on Christians, but also their destruction of ancient manuscripts, religious symbols, relics, monasteries and Church structures.

Their attempt is to destroy and remove anything Christian and that which they determine is contrary to or inconsistent with the teachings of the Koran. They are relentless in their pursuit and have used intimidation and fear tactics to accomplish their goal. If ISIS became a dominant movement in the United States, what would you do? Would you be willing and ready to die for your professed faith in Jesus Christ? Would your commitment and testimony be in the words of Paul, "I eagerly expect and hope that I will in no way be ashamed, but will have sufficient courage so that now as always Christ will be exalted in my body, whether by life or by death. For to me, to live is Christ and to die is gain" (Philippians 1:20-21, NIV)? Would you embrace and accept the admonition that states, "Whatever happens, conduct yourselves in a manner worthy of the gospel of Christ. Then, whether I come and see you or only hear about you in my absence, I will know that you stand firm in the one Spirit, striving together as one for the faith of the gospel without being frightened in any way by those who oppose you" (Philippians 1:27-28, NIV)?

The visible Church is supposed to be a true reflection of the Invisible Church, the Bride of the Lord Jesus Christ. One does not need to be a Church Historian to conclude that the visible Church is in turmoil and major denominations are assuming positions that are antithetical to that which is contained in the inspired Word of God. The message of the Church must be undiluted by the desires or perversions of the culture. The defining issues of right and wrong, righteousness and wickedness, godliness and ungodliness remain as God intended them to be. The distinction has always been God's Law or lawlessness; walking in the Spirit or walking in the things of the flesh; obedience to God and His Word or embracing some lesser alternative devised by mankind. Throughout the decades of the Billy Graham Evangelistic Crusades, the emphasis of Billy Graham as he proclaimed the Word was frequently stated and repeated, "The Bible says!" The visible Church needs to embrace and proclaim the same message in and to a hostile world. Will confrontations and challenges confront the Church as it does its

THE TWENTY-FIRST CENTURY CHURCH: IS IT WAXING OR WANING

Biblical ministry? Will opposition and resistance to those words being used ("The Bible says") become more pronounced? Will those who attempt the tactic of fear and intimidation to silence the message of God's Word become more vocal and physical? The answer to all of these questions is, Yes! In his book, Radical, David Platt wrote:

> Imagine all the blinds closed on the windows of a dimly lit room. Twenty leaders from different Churches in the area sat in a circle on the floor with their Bibles open. Some of them had sweat on their foreheads after walking for miles to get there. Others were dirty from the dust in the villages from which they had set out on bikes early that morning. They had gathered in secret. They had intentionally come to this place at different times throughout the morning so as not to draw attention to the meeting that was occurring. They lived in a country in Asia where it is illegal for them to gather like this. If caught, they could lose their land, their jobs, their families, or their lives.

This is the price some willingly pay to honor Jesus Christ, in order to know Him and to endeavor to make Him known. Are you willing to run any kind of risk today because of your personal commitment to Jesus Christ and His Word? Will you be a contributing part of the 21st Century Church that is waxing, or will you allow yourself to be marginalized and become identified with the Church that is waning? A hymn written by Albert B. Simpson (1891) asks an important question that deserves an answer by each of us (stanzas 2 and 3):

> *Jesus is standing on trial still,*
> *You can be false to Him if you will,*
> *You can be faithful through good or ill:*
> *What will you do with Jesus?*

> *Will you evade him as Pilate tried?*
> *Or will you choose Him, whatever betide?*
> *Vainly you struggle from Him to hide:*

James Perry

What will you do with Jesus?

The Refrain

What will you do with Jesus?
Neutral you cannot be;
Some day your heart will be asking,
What will He do with me?

15. Defining Thoughts

As you ponder your answer and commitment to the theme and question of this book, *The Twenty-First Century Church: Is It Waxing Or Waning?* we should also consider the price Jesus Christ paid to redeem you so that you could have eternal life through Him. Someone posted the following on Facebook (April 10, 2015).

> Almost 2000 years ago our redemption was secured by Christ's death on the cross. There he suffered not only the wrath of God, but the wrath of a humanist judicial system and a rebellious Israel, his own people. We are seeing today the continuing tendency of a humanist justice system, wherein men call evil good, and good evil and substitute darkness for light and light for darkness, Isaiah 5:20-21, "Woe to those who call evil good, and good evil; Who substitute darkness for light and light for darkness; Who substitute bitter for sweet and sweet for bitter! Woe to those who are wise in their own eyes And clever in their own sight!" The Christian faith is being persecuted not only by the humanism controlling our government but partly due to the failure of the modern Church to stand up for righteousness.

In 1982, Dr. C. Truman Davis wrote about the suffering and death of Jesus Christ in a paper: The Anatomical and Physiological Details of Death By Crucifixion. His paper included:

> Crucifixion was invented by the Persians in 300 BC, and perfected by the Romans in 100 BC. At the scourging of Jesus, His hands were tied to a post. Those responsible

for the scourging used a whip with 7 leather strips. To make the suffering greater and the damage more serious, two small lead balls were sharpened and tied to the ends of each leather strip so that they would cut deeply into the flesh. Scourging had the potential to kill the victim, because of the violence that was inflicted. The art of the torture was to bring someone close to the point of death, without having him expire. It is the most painful death ever invented by man and is where we get our term excruciating.

About the actual Crucifixion, he wrote:

1. The crucifixion of Jesus guaranteed a slow, painful death.
2. Being nailed to the Cross, Jesus had an impossible anatomical position to maintain.
3. His knees were flexed at about 45 degrees, and He was forced to bear His weight with the muscles of His Legs. It is not an anatomical position which is possible to maintain for more than a few minutes without severe cramps in the muscles of the thigh and calf.
4. His weight was borne on His feet, with nails driven through them.
5. As the strength of the muscles of Jesus' lower limbs tired, the weight of His body had to be transferred to His wrists, His arms, and His shoulders.
6. Within a few minutes of being placed on the Cross, Jesus' shoulders had become dislocated.
7. Minutes later, His elbows and wrists became dislocated.
The Prophecy was being fulfilled - Psalm 22:14,
"I am poured out like water, and all My bones are out of joint."
8. After His wrists, elbows and shoulders were dislocated, the weight of His body on his upper limbs causing

traction forces on the Pectoral-is Major muscles of His chest wall.

9. In order to breathe out, Jesus had to push down on the nails in His feet to raise His body, and allow His rib cage to move downwards and inwards to exhale air from His lungs.

10. The process of respiration caused excruciating pain, mixed with the reality of asphyxiation.

11. His movements up and down the Cross to breathe caused added excruciating pain in His wrist, His feet, and His dislocated elbows and shoulders.

12. He was covered in blood and sweat.
The blood was a result of the Crown of Thorns and The Scourging. The Sweat as a result of His involuntary attempts to exhale air from His lungs.

13. His physiological reflexes demanded that He took deeper breaths…

14. Due to His being nailed on the Cross and His increasing exhaustion, He was unable to provide more oxygen to His oxygen-starved body.

15. His heart beat faster and faster, and His pulse rate accelerated to about 220 beats/minute, the maximum normally sustainable.

16. Jesus had nothing to drink for 15 hours, since 6 pm the previous evening. He was already very dehydrated, and His blood pressure fell alarmingly. Probably about 80/50 He was in First Degree Shock

17. By about noon, His heart would've begun to fail.

18. His breathing was severely compromised.

19. He was in heart failure and respiratory failure.

20. Jesus said, "I thirst" because His body was crying out for fluids.

21. He was in desperate need of an intravenous infusion of blood and plasma to save His life

22. He could not breathe properly and was slowly suffocating to death.
23. Plasma and blood gathered in the space around His heart, called the Pericardium.
24. Because of the increasing physiological demands on His heart, He probably sustained Cardiac Rupture. His heart literally burst. This was probably the cause of His death.
25. At three o'clock in the afternoon Jesus said, "It is finished."
26. At that moment, He gave up His Spirit, and He died - after six hours of the most excruciating and terrifying torture ever invented.
27. Jesus died to secure everlasting life for His people whom He had come to seek and to save.
28. He died so that ordinary people like you and me could go to His Heaven.

As Charles Wesley contemplated the suffering and death of Jesus Christ, he wrote the words to a seldom sung hymn (1742):

O Love divine, what hast thou done!
The immortal God hath died for me!
The Father's co-eternal Son
bore all my sins upon the tree.
The immortal God for me hath died:
My Lord, my Love, is crucified!

Is crucified for me and you,
to bring us rebels back to God.
Believe, believe the record true,
ye all are bought with Jesus' blood.
Pardon for all flows from his side:
My Lord, my Love, is crucified!

THE TWENTY-FIRST CENTURY CHURCH: IS IT WAXING OR WANING

At this point, the issue of Fidelity versus Falderal (discussed in Chapter 14) comes to the forefront. Fidelity here refers to the terms of the actual death of Jesus Christ. Falderal would discount and discredit who Jesus was and what Jesus claims He would do and actually did. Following the scourging and crucifixion, the only conclusion of Christ's followers was that Jesus Is Dead! They have watched His scourging! They have seen His suffering! They have observed His anguish on the cross! They have heard His last words, "It Is Finished! Into Your hands I commend/commit My spirit!" They have seen His body placed in the tomb of Joseph of Arimathea! They have seen the large stone rolled into place at the entrance to the tomb! They had learned about the Chief Priests and Scribes request made to Pilate (Matthew 27:62-68)! They have heard about the seal that has been affixed on that stone at the entrance of the tomb! They know a sentry is guarding the place where Jesus lay! The mood and atmosphere among the disciples and friends is one of sorrow and emptiness. Judas, the Betrayer, had committed suicide by hanging himself! The disciples were hiding and fearful! Close friends of Jesus were sad and mourning! They concluded that the enemies of Jesus had triumphed! They are left without their Leader! What are they to do now?

The disciples and other followers had forgotten or failed to comprehend the words Jesus had spoken in their midst about His death and resurrection. Fidelity to the Word of God would cause one to embrace the words of Jesus.

> I am the resurrection and the life; he who believes in Me will live even if he dies, and everyone who lives and believes in Me will never die. Do you believe this?
> (Earlier Jesus had stated this in the presence of the Pharisees (The Parable of The Good Shepherd and His Sheep). John 11:25-26

James Perry

> The reason my Father loves me is that I lay down my life only to take it up again. No one takes it from me, but I lay it down of my own accord. I have authority to lay it down and authority to take it up again. This command I received from my Father. John 10:17-18

> A little while, and you will no longer see Me; and again a little while, and you will see Me...Truly, truly, I say to you, that you will weep and lament, but the world will rejoice; you will grieve, but your grief will be turned into joy...I will see you again, and your heart will rejoice, and no one will take your joy away from you. (Jesus had said To His Disciples) John 16:16-22

If the resurrection of Jesus Christ had not occurred, all of His previous words spoken would be null and void. They would be rejected by those who opposed Jesus as well as by those who followed Him. However, Matthew 28:1-7 records that a severe earthquake had occurred. The women who had come to the tomb on the first day of the week saw an angel seated on the stone that had been rolled away. The angel said to the women, Do not be afraid; for I know that you are looking for Jesus who has been crucified. He is not here, for He has risen, just as He said. This event so captivated the heart and mind of The Apostle Paul that he exuberantly wrote, "Paul, a servant of Jesus Christ, who was declared to be the Son of God with power by the resurrection from the dead, according to the Spirit of holiness, Jesus Christ our Lord" (Romans 1:4). He would go on to write in I Corinthians 15 about all of the eyewitnesses and proofs of the literal resurrection of Jesus Christ. He emphasized that faith and hope are the reality for the follower of Jesus Christ because He arose from the dead and is alive forevermore. It gives the basis and credence to the heartfelt confidence of Horatio C. Spafford (1873). Following two sorrowful experiences in his life, the Chicago Fire of 1871 that ruined him financially and the death of his four daughters in a ship collision while they were crossing the Atlantic, in the midst of his personal sorrow, he penned the words to a hymn that included"

My sin—oh, the bliss of this glorious thought!—
My sin, not in part but the whole,
Is nailed to the cross, and I bear it no more,
Praise the Lord, praise the Lord, O my soul!

Refrain:

It is well with my soul,
It is well, it is well with my soul.

As the Apostle Paul reflected on the power and reality of the resurrection, he would write of his personal longing and fervent desire (Philippians 3:10-11).

> I want to know Him (Jesus Christ) and the power of His resurrection and the fellowship of His sufferings, being conformed to His death; in order that I may attain to the resurrection from the dead.

The reality for the Twenty-First Century Church as it straddles the proverbial fence between waxing or waning is to know the amazing power of the resurrection, and thereby to know the amazing Savior Who died and rose again. Do you know Him and His power in and for your life? Are you certain you will be going to His heaven to live with Him for eternity? You can know by actuating Romans 10:8-10, 13.

> The Word is in your mouth and in your heart, that is, the word of faith which we are preaching, that if you confess with your mouth Jesus is Lord, and believe in your heart that God raised Him from the dead, you will be saved; for with the heart a person believes, resulting in

righteousness, and with the mouth he confesses, resulting in salvation...For whoever will call on the name of The Lord will be saved.

If this is your confession and belief, you have the assurance that your salvation is eternal life in Jesus Christ. A Biblical truth that one must grasp, understand and believe is recorded in I John 5:9-13 (ESV).

This is the testimony of God that he has borne concerning his Son. Whoever believes in the Son of God has the testimony in himself. Whoever does not believe God has made him a liar, because he has not believed in the testimony that God has borne concerning his Son. And this is the testimony, that God gave us eternal life, and this life is in his Son. Whoever has the Son has life; whoever does not have the Son of God does not have life. I write these things to you who believe in the name of the Son of God that you may know that you have eternal life.

Despite the evil, wickedness and chaos that prevails in the world, the foundational truth of eternal life in Jesus Christ fills us with hope. A devotional in *Our Daily Bread* for April 24, 2015 is titled, "Hope Lives." It contains these words of encouragement for those who are walking faithfully with the Lord, "Peter...praises God for our new birth into a living hope through our salvation. That hope can bring joy even in the middle of tragedy. He also assures us of the permanence of this hope. He then tells us of the heart-breaking reality that we may suffer grief in all kinds of trials. Those who have suffered loss turn hopeful hearts toward Peter's next words: These come so that your faith . . . may be found to praise, honor, and glory at the revelation of Jesus Christ" (1Peter 1:3-7, NIV). You can know these truths as your reality today. This reality has been summed up in the beautiful words of the hymn,

THE TWENTY-FIRST CENTURY CHURCH: IS IT WAXING OR WANING

Loved with everlasting love,
Led by grace that love to know;
Spirit, breathing from above,
Thou hast taught me it is so.
Oh, this full and perfect peace! O
h, this transport all divine!
In a love which cannot cease,
I am His, and He is mine.
(George Wade Robinson - 1836-1877)

I am challenged by the words written by Charles Wesley in 1740 as he reflected on the Cross of Jesus Christ. He was convicted by his own sin and life not being lived in greater compliance with God's love. mercy and grace. His wrote his thoughts and words in a lengthy Hymn (13 stanzas) that included,

Depth of mercy! Can there be
Mercy still reserved for me?
Can my God His wrath forbear,
Me, the chief of sinners, spare?

I have long withstood His grace,
Long provoked Him to His face,
Would not hearken to His calls,
Grieved Him by a thousand falls.

I my Master have denied,
I afresh have crucified,
And profaned His hallowed Name,
Put Him to an open shame.

If I rightly read Thy heart,
If Thou all compassion art,
Bow Thine ear, in mercy bow,

James Perry

Pardon and accept me now.

Now incline me to repent,
Let me now my sins lament,
Now my foul revolt deplore,
Weep, believe, and sin no more.

16. Authoritarian Domination

After they had stopped speaking, James answered, saying, Brethren, listen to me. Simeon has related how God first concerned Himself about taking from among the Gentiles a people for His name. With this the words of the Prophets agree...Therefore it is my judgment that we do not trouble those who are turning to God from among the Gentiles, but that we write to them that they abstain from things contaminated by idols and from fornication and from what is strangled and from blood.
Acts 15:13-20 (Selected - NASB)

One of the greatest hindrances within the visible Church in the twenty-first century is an internal power structure that develops. The general attitude of most people within a local Church is to go along in order to get along. It is borne out of apathy and some degree of detachment from the processes within the developing power base. If left unchecked, it can allow for the emergence of men who can become reckless and ruthless as their personal authority is permitted or ignored. The downside to this development is that the will of God is usually set aside and the will of man becomes dominant. What is necessary for a local Church to regain its focus and God-ordained principles for His Church?

A theme posted by Josh Hunt in his Blog is on the necessity for Discipleship *(http://www.joshhunt.com/2014/10/05/two-questions-to-ask-if-your-Church-is-in-decline/)*. He suggests two questions that should be considered and researched if a particular Church is in a state of decline.

> In taking an objective evaluation of your ministry setting perhaps two of the questions to begin with are, 1) What happened leading up to the point at which decline became visible? 2) What did the organization do in the

wake of this visible evidence? The answer to the first question most often has to do with a financial shortage or a loss of key lay leaders in the Church. Until there comes a shortage of financial resources or manpower to carry out ministry many Church leaders ignore the signs of decline. The second question is designed to allow Church leaders to draw on retrospect of actions taken or the lack of action...Churches that have been in decline for several years have a tendency to gradually move to what I refer to as a turned-in mentality (not reaching or benefiting the community). One line of questioning I have used at times is to ask for the thoughts of Church members and leaders on what are the strengths of the Church. (What is the Church good at doing?)...Normally the trend is most if not all of perceived strengths in a declining Church are for the Church members, not the community or the lost world...

As I reflected on the thoughts shared in Josh Hunt's Blog, I wrote the following response:

"I have a slight amplification to your two stated actions...They are: (1) The denial of demographic changes (include a subtle refusal to accept things as they are) and ignoring (sometimes blatantly refusing) any interest in cross-cultural ministry. (2) The internal power structure determining that the Pastor must be removed and replaced (in the hope that a younger man with a growing family will become a magnet that will attract other younger families to their Church) is based upon fiction more than fact. It's a cosmetic approach that soon tapers off and the decline continues. Also - many Churches fail in other areas. One prevailing area is the failure to take a serious God seriously. Another prevailing area is when the leadership is lacking perception and commitment to the invisible Church so

THE TWENTY-FIRST CENTURY CHURCH:
IS IT WAXING OR WANING

that it will become more visible and viable in the local Church. Unless and until that happens, decline will continue in the visible Church and it will model waning rather than waxing.

When I completed my seminary training, I had been well-trained and prepared for serving the Lord as a Pastor or in some other aspect of Christian Ministry. One of the professors would remind his students, unless "Woe is me if I preach not the Gospel" is burning in your bones, then seek some other vocation. This challenge impressed me and I felt a degree of the passion expressed by the Apostle Paul in Romans 1:14-16, "I am obligated…I am so eager to preach the gospel…I am not ashamed of the gospel, because it is the power of God that brings salvation to everyone who believes." Following graduation in 1964, my wife and children and I , with great expectation and enthusiasm, left for our first pastorate. The expectation and enthusiasm would soon fade with the reality that this was not shared by most in the congregation. They saw their Church as a challenge greater than their capability to maintain or expand. Their vision for ministry was minimal and the reason for their existence was inexplicable.

Two impressions were made upon me at the outset of being a pastor. The first impression was during my ordination service. The man who preached the sermon made a statement that startled me. He said, "You will find that some people you trust and care for the most will be among the first who plunge a dagger into your back and twist it while doing so." Sadly, throughout more than fifty years of ministry, I have seen that occur time and time again. The many smaller Churches have similarity in that they think short-term pastorates will serve them best. The short-sightedness on their part is that it prevents momentum in ministry. They tend to think that a new broom will sweep clean. The subtlety is that they realize the old broom has learned where the dirt is located. The second impression was when two senior Pastors took time to visit me as a younger Pastor in a challenging and difficult Church situation. One of them shared with me, "The ideals that you have for ministry are correct and good." He then added, "Just put those ideals in your hip pocket, never forget where they are or what they represent, but realize that people in the Church will do what they can to prevent you from putting those ideals (values) into effective use." This comment was prophetic and could've served as commentary about several other Churches.

So often, too often, a "Mr. Big" in a congregation will be the proverbial "tail that wags the dog." If a man chooses to attempt ministry apart from his stamp of approval, it will be met by resistance. Everyone will soon learn whether or not "Mr. Big" gave his tacit approval. If not, the pastor who proceeds with his ministry vision will do so to his own demise. The pastor will be asked to move on so that the peace, purity and unity of the Church can be preserved. However, "Mr. Big" will still be there and exercise his will when the next servant of the Lord comes and attempts to do ministry in "Mr. Big's" Church. The cycle will then begin once again when "Mr. Big" and some of his ilk become dissatisfied with the Pastor.

There seems to be no limit to the vitriol, vindictiveness and viciousness that can flow from so-called Church leaders toward a Pastor. I know of one Church where it was a criticism of the Pastor's appearance. In another Church, a man who had tried to serve a small congregation as faithfully as he could, was subjected regularly to criticism for not being more friendly and effective. When it was mutually agreed upon that the pastor would move elsewhere, he felt assured that verbal abuse would be ended. As his possessions from the Church and his home were almost completely loaded on the moving van, the most vocal of men who had spoken so harshly to and about the Pastor, came to inspect the premises. In doing so, he was unable to find the copier that belonged to the Church. He accused the Pastor of stealing it and demanded that everything be unloaded from the Moving Van until it was located it. To accomplish this deed, he called the local Police to come and oversee what he had demanded. One man who had been attending the Church was a State Highway Trooper. When he heard the police band radio dispatch, he drove to the Church to determine what was happening. After being told, the State Trooper approached the gathered group of Church leaders and told them that he and the pastor had moved the copier to his home for safe-keeping. Despite the moment of chagrin, the men never apologized to the departing pastor nor was there any attempt for reconciliation.

In another Church, despite the fact that there was marginal growth, a group of "power brokers" were fearful that the "outsiders" would take over their Church property. Regardless of facts to the contrary, these men refused to reconcile with the pastor and went to a local court to secure a legal order to remove the man from both the Church-owned home and the Church building. They prevailed and won the court injunction against the young pastor. It was a sad day to see the county Sheriff standing at the Church door as the man and his library were removed from the Church building. No thought was given concerning the reproach brought to the name of Jesus Christ! Strong-willed men carried out their will in terms of their Church. All of this contributed to the young man leaving the ministry. Additionally, the Church was not favorably viewed by the community. The men who won the court battle lost relevance in the community and as a Church. The Church building is not only an exhibit of waning and a building in disrepair but the congregation has also waned and is down to less than a handful of people.

The men who sought a court injunction, even though they were contacted by a former pastor about seeking biblical reconciliation, ignored the counsel. The former pastor had shared the biblical admonition they should read and apply, I Corinthians 6:1-9 (NLT).

When one of you has a dispute with another believer,

how dare you file a lawsuit and ask a secular court to decide the matter instead of taking it to other believers! Don't you realize that someday we believers will judge the world? And since you are going to judge the world, can't you decide even these little things among yourselves? Don't you realize that we will judge angels? So you should surely be able to resolve ordinary disputes in this life. If you have legal disputes about such matters, why go to outside judges who are not respected by the Church? I am saying this to shame you. Isn't there anyone in all the Church who is wise enough to decide these issues? But instead, one believer sues another—right in front of un-believers! Even to have such lawsuits with one another is a defeat for you. Why not just accept the injustice and leave it at that? Why not let yourselves be cheated? Instead, you yourselves are the ones who do wrong and cheat even your fellow believers. Don't you realize that those who do wrong will not inherit the Kingdom of God? Don't fool yourselves.

These men could not and would not change their decision. It became a type of obsession with them and with a determination to win at any cost.

Another criticism often stated is that the Pastor doesn't visit the members of the congregation often enough. Of course, "Mr. Big" and his companions seldom put forth any effort to visit or assist in the overall ministry. In one Church, Evangelism Training was being done and an out-reach effort was going to be scheduled. However, "Mr. Big" had his idea for evangelism and at the last session, handed out Booklets that he wanted used. The result was that weeks of training was thwarted and the Pastor received the criticism for the Evangelism plan not getting implemented. Even after "Mr. Big" dies, his memory casts a large shadow over future ministry. A reputation soon attaches itself to a local Church and it is similar to an albatross that hangs upon one's neck. One man stated his reason for not attending

THE TWENTY-FIRST CENTURY CHURCH:
IS IT WAXING OR WANING

the local Church was that anyone doing so would have to show their bank statement first. These types of illustrations are endless. The behavior of a few is subtle and devious but a very real circumstance that causes a Church to be waning rather than the waxing. It should not be surprising to learn that Pastors will sometimes become discouraged. He may reach a point of frustration where he gives up and goes into some other task outside of ministry.

I am personally challenged by the overall attitude of the Church today and whether or not it is taking a serious God seriously. On April 20, 2015, *The Thriving Pastor* (produced by Focus On The Family and written by Kevin Conklin,. *http://blog thrivingpastor.com*) included the following summary and statistics:

> When I read the statistics of how many Pastors quit/resign or are fired on an annual basis, it burdens me to near sleeplessness. And when you throw in the excessive number of pastors who are so fatigued, tired, and burned out that they're barely surviving, well it could get depressing. Here's some information from a study by Dr. Richard J. Krejcir from the Francis A. Shaeffer Institute of Church Leadership and Development (2007 Statistics on Pastors):
>
> 28% of pastors read the Bible for personal enjoyment vs. only for study/sermon preparation.
>
> 38% are either divorced or in the process of divorce.
>
> 70% admitted to having no close personal friend or confidant.
>
> 77% did not feel like they had a good or satisfying marriage.

71% felt burned out, fatigued, and fighting depression on a weekly or even daily basis.

30% admitted to either being in, or having been in, a sexual affair while in ministry.

Temptation itself isn't a sin, but for some reason hardly anyone talks about it openly and honestly as if talking about it were sin itself. Looking at James 1:13-16 we can clearly see the progression of temptation to sin, but for some reason people who give into temptation can't seem to find their way out and never feel safe enough to be held accountable.

During the years of our marriage (nearing 60 years), my wife and I have been in agreement about the basics of commitment and what it entails for us to be walking with the Lord. For us, they include:

> Proverbs 3:5-7 - Trust in the Lord with all your heart and do not lean on your own understanding. In all your ways acknowledge Him, and He will make your paths straight. Do not be wise in your own eyes; Fear the LORD and turn away from evil.
> To viably trust in the Lord means:
> - All our heart
> - Not leaning on our understanding
> - Acknowledging the Lord in all of our ways
> - Not being wise in our own eyes
> - Fearing and reverencing the Lord always, and
> - Turning away from every evil way
>
> Psalm 37:3-7 - Trust in the Lord and do good; Dwell in the land and cultivate faithfulness. Delight yourself in the Lord; And He will give you the desires of your heart.

THE TWENTY-FIRST CENTURY CHURCH: IS IT WAXING OR WANING

Commit your way to the Lord, Trust also in Him, and He will do it. He will bring forth your righteousness as the light And your judgment as the noonday. Rest in the Lord and wait patiently for Him; Do not fret because of him who prospers in his way, Because of the man who carries out wicked schemes.

The key steps and factors are: Trust; Cultivation of faithfulness; Delighting in the Lord; Committing our way to the Lord; Resting and relaxing in Him; Waiting patiently for Him and His timing; and Not fretting (becoming or being anxious) about details and the small "stuff."

Proverbs 16:3 - Commit your works to the Lord and your plans will be established.

Psalm 37:5 emphasized: Commit our WAY (where we are going or heading), whereas Proverbs 16:3 places the emphasis on: Commit our WORK (what we are doing or aspiring to do).

Psalm 37:23-27 - The steps of a man are established by the Lord, And He delights in his way. When he falls, he will not be hurled headlong, Because the Lord is the One who holds his hand. I have been young and now I am old, Yet I have not seen the righteous forsaken or his descendants begging bread. All day long he is gracious and lends, And his descendants are a blessing. The issue is whether or not we are prepared to seek first the Kingdom of God and His righteousness. If we are, then assurance is given that all we need will be supplied and provided for us by our Heavenly Father (Matthew 6:33).

Proverbs 30:7-9 - Two things I asked of You, do not refuse me before I die: Keep deception and lies far from me, Give me neither poverty nor riches; Feed me with the food that is my portion, that I not be full and deny You and say, Who is the Lord? Or that I not be in want and steal, and profane the name of my God.

The Balance must be found between what we want and that which is a basic need. It means our being content with God's provisions for us.

The idea of serving the Lord at any time, in any place, to do any work at any cost seems lost by many younger Pastors entering ministry. There is often a Pay Package negotiation that seems to be Priority One rather than the definite call of God to be engaged in a Pastoral Care Ministry in the place that is seeking a shepherd for the flock. The focus should be on the lost or straying sheep and a strategy for reaching out to the lost and wandering souls in the community. The Lord will provide for His faithful servants.

Peter had learned a valuable lesson regarding ministry priorities and responsibilities from a personal interaction with Jesus Christ (John 21:15-23). There were two major thrusts, how much do you love Me and how well do you love Me? If you love Me as you say you do, then accept the responsibility to feed and care for My lambs and sheep. It is obvious that Peter accepted and acted upon those priorities and responsibilities. There is the unique application of these principles when Peter wrote to a persecuted Church, (I Peter 5:1-3, ESV).

> So I exhort the elders among you, as a fellow elder and a witness of the sufferings of Christ, as well as a partaker in the glory that is going to be revealed: shepherd the flock of God that is among you, exercising oversight, not under compulsion, but willingly, as God would have you; not for shameful gain, but eagerly; not domineering over those in your charge, but being examples to the flock.

THE TWENTY-FIRST CENTURY CHURCH: IS IT WAXING OR WANING

Peter's points are very clear. The flock of God requires faithful shepherding, leading and feeding. The Shepherd is to provide this care and oversight willingly. He is not to be preoccupied with shameful gain (pay packages) but to serve with eagerness. He is to be kindhearted, merciful and patient. He must remember that the sheep and lambs in his care are not to be driven like cattle but be led into the pastures where they will be nourished. There is no place or room for those who would seek to infiltrate the flock with their authoritarian domination. That intrusion and influence would result in the flock waning (diminishing) rather than waxing (nourished and growing).

The idea of sheep and lambs is emphasized in Scriptural passages such as Psalm 23 and John 10. It also has found its way into Hymns that have been written. In 1836, Dorothy A Thrupp wrote the words that are often referred to as a Children's Hymn. However, the words have a much broader application for all those who are included in the flock of our God and Savior, Jesus Christ. The words serve as a prayer of the sheep or lambs speaking to the Shepherd of the flock. It can serve as a purposeful prayer for us today. May you faithfully follow The Shepherd always!

Savior, like a shepherd lead us,
much we need Thy tender care;
In Thy pleasant pastures feed us,
for our use Thy folds prepare.
Blessed Jesus, blessed Jesus!
Thou hast bought us, Thine we are.

We are Thine, Thou dost befriend us,
be the guardian of our way;
Keep Thy flock, from sin defend us,
seek us when we go astray.
Blessed Jesus, blessed Jesus! Hear,
O hear us when we pray.

James Perry

*Now may the God of peace who brought again from the dead our
Lord Jesus,
the great shepherd of the sheep,
by the blood of the eternal covenant,
equip you with everything good
that you may do his will,
working in us that which is pleasing in his sight,
through Jesus Christ,
to whom be glory forever and ever.
Amen.
(Hebrews 13:20-21, ESV)*

17. An Accurate Epitaph

A lawyer stood up to put him to the test, saying, Teacher, what shall I do to inherit eternal life? He said to him, What is written in the Law? How do you read it? And he answered, You shall love the Lord your God with all your heart and with all your soul and with all your strength and with all your mind, and your neighbor as yourself. And he said to him, You have answered correctly; do this, and you will live.
Luke 10:25-28 (ESV)

After this I looked, and there before me was a great multitude that no one could count, from every nation, tribe, people and language, standing before the throne and before the Lamb. They were wearing white robes and were holding palm branches in their hands. And they cried out in a loud voice: Salvation belongs to our God, who sits on the throne, and to the Lamb.
Revelation 7:9-10 (NIV)

All kinds of epitaphs have been written in an attempt to briefly characterize the death of a person. John Newton's tombstone has his testimony etched upon it: "John Newton, Clerk, once an infidel and libertine, a servant of slaves in Africa, was, by the rich mercy of our Lord and Savior Jesus Christ, preserved, restored, pardoned, and appointed to preach the faith he had long labored to destroy"(http://www.gospelweb.net/JohnNewton/newtontombstone.htm). If an epitaph was being written about the twenty-first century Church, what summary would be given? If you were given that responsibility, what would you write? In preparing that epitaph, a question to consider would be: Is the twenty-first century Church vibrant and healthy or is it diminished, failing and in its death throes? What if you were writing your own epitaph as a Biblical Christian, what would you want it to convey?

In Chapter 16, statistics were listed about Pastors and Churches. The summary and statistics can be a determining factor in terms of Church health and the direction it is heading. One of the contributing factors pertaining to the health of the Pastor is his lack of accountability. A Pastor may give sermons on how others should be accountable while shielding himself from a similar process. There needs to be an assessment in terms of why a Pastor is leaving Church A so he can go to Church B. Was there some personality conflict issues? Was the Pastor indifferent to the needs of the congregation and community? Did he lack leadership skills? Was he accessible to his congregation? Did he locate a different Church that would pay him a higher salary? How much time was given to prayer as he sought God's will and direction for his life and ministry? Was the pastor being besieged by some strong natural leader types? Were they dictating how they wanted "their Church" operated and what they wanted "their Pastor" (and his family) to be and do? Any Pastor and Church would do well to read The Book of Acts as and when any consideration for present and future ministry is contemplated. There you will find when the best efforts of the Apostles were refused or rejected, they would follow the Holy Spirit's direction for their lives and move to another location to continue ministry.

A larger issue was addressed in a sermon given by John Piper in 2002 on, "My Anguish: My Kinsmen Are Accursed." The content of that sermon was directed to the alteration of basic Biblical Doctrine and why it was being altered. One of his emphases was:

> There is a sad irony in the seeming success of many Christian Churches and schools. The irony is that the more you adjust obscure Biblical doctrines to make Christian reality more attractive to unbelievers, the less Christian reality there is when they arrive. Which means that what looks like success in the short run, may, in the long run, prove to be failure. If you alter or obscure the

THE TWENTY-FIRST CENTURY CHURCH: IS IT WAXING OR WANING

Biblical portrait of God in order to attract converts, you don't get converts to God, you get converts to an illusion. This is not evangelism, but deception…Many observers today are making note that what the liberal mainline Churches did 60 years ago, evangelical Churches are doing today. The mainstream Christian Churches are declining in popularity, and the conservative Protestant Churches are losing their doctrinal and behavioral distinctiveness. There are thousands of pastors and Churches today that do not think that clear, Biblical, doctrinal views are vital in the life of the Church or the believer. They believe it is possible to grow a healthy Church while leaving the people with few and fuzzy thoughts about what God is like. But ignorance about God is never a mere vacuum. The cavity created by ignorance fills up with something else.

Could these words by John Piper be the epitaph for the Twenty-First Century Church? Are his words indicating that the Church today is waxing or waning? In case you have a doubt, his statement: "The mainstream Christian Churches are declining in popularity, and the conservative Protestant Churches are losing their doctrinal and behavioral distinctiveness" indicates that it is waning (descending) rather than waxing (ascending).

All kinds of calamity can occur when there is adjustment to Biblical doctrine within the Church and the belief system of professing Christians. Have you considered the ramifications for a visible Church, a professing Christian, a culture or a nation that no longer sees the need for or makes room to include Jehovah God as part and parcel of a way of life? It is obvious in the United States of America that the process of eliminating God as a focal point in its way of life began more than fifty years ago. The long range goal to remove prayer and Bible reading from the public schools, as well as the shift to remove Manger Scenes from the public square and the singing of Christmas Carols, all serve as a trend toward cultural inclinations and enslavement. The legalization of abortion and same-gender marriages are subtly designed to further adjust Biblical doctrine and teaching in the public arena. It is sad to observe mainstream Churches either naively or gullibly going along with the adjustment of Biblical doctrine. For some, it is a complete abdication of Biblical teaching and Scriptural authority.

What if the culture made an absolute decision that God was no longer wanted or welcomed in the life of the nation or community, what would you think? What would you do? What if you personally reached a decision that God was unnecessary for your life and you did not need to depend upon Him for anything at any time, how do you think that would impact your life? I want us to think about the possibility of God being exiled from our lives and culture. Let us also think about Him being more of an unwanted intrusion rather than an absolute necessity for our daily lives, our liberties and the unlimited pursuit of happiness. What would life be like without God and His Standards?

Let's pursue a thumbnail sketch in the Biblical History of God seeking His people and where the choice of life without God was tried in different generations. We begin with the Garden of Eden where the most unique relationship of God with His created beings took place. The Genesis record indicates that God came in the cool of every evening seeking out Adam and Eve to have personal and intimate fellowship with them. This continued for an extended period of time until Adam and Eve decided an alternative life-plan would be better for them. Their choice was horrendous inasmuch as it plunged the entire universe into alienation from God, the Creator (Romans 5:12-13). The only resolve for mankind is a determined choice to seek after the provision and work of God's grace, (See: Romans 5:15-17). This passage represents the amazing grace of the amazing God provided through the amazing Savior, Jesus Christ, so that in Him God's amazing redemption would be realized and actuated in our lives: "Therefore, having been justified by faith, we have peace with God through our Lord Jesus Christ, through whom also we have obtained our introduction by faith into this grace in which we stand; and we exult in hope of the glory of God" (Romans 5:1-2)!

The lessons about relationship and fellowship with the Eternal God are not easily learned. The obvious is not always embraced by those who think they know what is best or better for their lives. For them, God seems remote and inconsequential. An example of this is when Moses was led the children of Israel out from their bondage in Egypt. They had the unique privilege of seeing God's power as His plagues impacted the Egyptian people. At the point when they began their journey away from Egypt, God gave them a visible sign of His continued presence with them and His care for them. A great cloud (Shekinah Glory Cloud) led them by day through the wilderness. Additionally, there was a pillar of fire that provided them with both light for the night hours as well as protection from all potential dangers. The people soon wearied of the daily heavenly provision of Manna for their dietary needs. They allowed themselves to look back at the food they were able to eat while they were enslaved in Egypt and they desired it once again. Are you able to perceive their discontentment with God? Can you imagine that you would ever be impatient with God, discontented with His provision for you and become weary of how He is supplying for your needs?

When the Tabernacle was built in the wilderness, provision was made for the permanent residence of God in the midst of His people. The place would be called the Holy of Holies. The Ark of the Covenant was placed there and served as the focal point for the children of Israel as the special community of God's people. It served to remind them of God's Laws and His expectations for His people. In time, the unthinkable happened. Israel lost God in their midst when they went out to fight the Philistines. The Israelites camped at Ebenezer ("thus far the Lord has helped us"). The Philistines deployed their forces to meet Israel, and as the battle spread, Israel was defeated by the Philistines, The elders of Israel asked: "Why did the Lord bring defeat on us today before the Philistines?" They decided that if they had the symbol of God's presence with them in the battle the result would have been victory rather than defeat. They sent a request to have the Ark of the Covenant brought into their encampment. When the Ark of the Covenant arrives, "All Israel raised such a great shout that the ground shook" (I Samuel 4:10, NIV). The Israelites were ecstatic and sensed "God with us" equates with we will now be victorious. A subtle issue for Israel is that they viewed the Ark of the Covenant more as a good luck charm rather than the actual presence of God in their midst. If they had adequately feared Him, obeyed Him and reverenced His name, the outcome would've been much different. Do you view the Holy God as a good luck charm? Do you view the Cross of Jesus Christ as something ornate for display or significant just as a piece of jewelry to be worn?

Using God only as a religious symbol, Israel carried the Ark of the Covenant into the renewed battle with the Philistines. Their confidence was high. They believed victory was imminent. To their dismay, the Philistines prevailed once again. Israel was defeated and every man fled. They had suffered a great loss and thirty-thousand of their foot soldiers had been killed in the conflict. On a personal basis, what would you do if you lost the presence of God? What would you do without Him? Where would you go to find Him? How diligently would you seek for Him? What risks would you take to find Him? When would you begin to look for Him? Do you think you would be able to survive without God? How long would you delay before you began your search? Would God be able to depend upon you to seek Him and find Him because you had searched for Him with all your heart and being?

The Philistines, due to the devastation throughout their land and tumors inflicting their people, decided to rid themselves of Israel's God. They sent the Ark of the Covenant to Gath but the people of Gath had the same experience of devastation and the spread of tumors. They decided to send it to Ekron. However, the news of the devastation and disease had become known and the people of Ekron rejected the Ark of the Covenant coming into their community. The possible solution for their dilemma is recorded in I Samuel 5:11-12, "Send the ark of the God of Israel away; let it go back to its own place, or it will kill us and our people. For death had filled the city with panic; God's hand was very heavy on it. Those who did not die were afflicted with tumors, and the outcry of the city went up to heaven." At this point, God was homeless. No one wanted God around or in their midst. He had been the source of devastation and disease. They decided to send Him away. They think that Israel will want their God back with them. The Philistines decided to put the Ark of God on a cart and send it back to Israel. The reasoning and rationale for this decision was given in I Samuel 6:5-13. The counsel that led them to make this decision was: "Perhaps God will lift his hand from you and your gods and your land."

A great moment for Israel soon resulted in disaster for them. The people of Beth Shemesh (house of the sun) were harvesting their wheat in the valley. When they looked up and saw the Ark, they rejoiced at the sight. It was a resounding expression of their joy and delight. However, some people foolishly and needlessly erred when they decided to look inside The Ark of the Covenant. I Samuel 6:19-21 indicates "God struck down some of the inhabitants and seventy of them died because they looked into the ark of the Lord. The people mourned because of the heavy blow the Lord had dealt them. And the people of Beth Shemesh asked, Who can stand in the presence of the Lord, this holy God?" They decided to send The Ark of the Covenant somewhere else, anywhere else, just to get it out of their community.

There is much more to this story of how the presence of God was undesirable for the communities that wanted to maintain their traditions and their customs. The presence of God would cramp their lifestyle. There are at least two major truths that should be gleaned about God and what He desires His people to be and do. The first is stated in I Peter 2:4-8 where Peter instructed the persecuted Church of his day, "As you come to him, the living Stone, rejected by humans but chosen by God and precious to him, you also, like living stones, are being built into a spiritual house to be a holy priesthood, offering spiritual sacrifices acceptable to God through Jesus Christ..." The thrust of the instruction is that we are to be (a) a spiritual house that is (b) offering spiritual sacrifices that are acceptable to God. A question to examine and act upon: Does the twenty-first century Church meet this requirement? Is it waxing or waning in terms of God's expectation for His people and His Church? What are the spiritual sacrifices being offered to God in the twenty-first century Church? An appropriate starting point is Romans 12:1-2 and acting upon the words of Paul,

> I urge you...in view of God's mercy, to offer your bodies as a living sacrifice, holy and pleasing to God—this is your true and proper worship. Do not conform to the pattern of this world, but be transformed by the renewing of your mind. Then you will be able to test and approve what God's will is—his good, pleasing and perfect will.

A personal choice and commitment is required by each of us. Have you made your choice to be a "living sacrifice" that is "holy and pleasing to God"? If you have answered positively to this question, it must become the regular practice of your life. It is a commitment to a daily way of life. This is amplified for us in Hebrews 13:15-16 (NIV), "Through Jesus...let us continually offer to God a sacrifice of praise, the fruit of lips that openly profess his name. And do not forget to do good and to share with others, for with such sacrifices God is pleased."

THE TWENTY-FIRST CENTURY CHURCH: IS IT WAXING OR WANING

When Peter wrote about the Biblical Christian becoming a spiritual house (I Peter 2:4-8), he is indicating that the spiritual house had actually become a spiritual temple. Paul had written about this truth in I Corinthians 3:16-17 (ESV), "Do you not know that you are God's temple and that God's Spirit dwells in you? If anyone destroys God's temple, God will destroy him. For God's temple is holy, and you are that temple." Paul repeated this thought in II Corinthians 6:16-18 (ESV), "What agreement has the temple of God with idols? For we are the temple of the living God; as God said, I will make my dwelling among them and walk among them, and I will be their God, and they shall be my people. Therefore go out from their midst, and be separate from them, says the Lord, and touch no unclean thing…says the Lord Almighty."

Do you have that sense of being God's holy temple? Do you reflect that truth by the way you live and the things you do? Is the Triune God a welcome resident in your body that is His Temple? Is your life being lived for His Glory?

Many Churches begin a worship service singing words based upon Habakkuk 2:20, that remind us: "The Lord is in his holy temple; let all the earth be silent before him." When the Psalmist reflected upon the presence of God among His people, he wrote (Psalm 11:4), "The Lord is in his holy temple; the Lord is on his heavenly throne. He observes everyone on earth; his eyes examine them." Is your personal life as a professing Christian, waxing or waning? Do observers recognize you are a spiritual house and a holy temple of the Lord? Is the visible Church you attend and in which you participate one that is waxing or waning? Does it radiate the presence of the glory of God or has that glory departed? In what ways is your Church vital and viable in the twenty-first century? Can it be said of your life that The Risen Lord is present in His Holy Temple? There is no substitute for consistency. The objective of both the visible Church and Biblical Christian will be a commitment that all things will be done for God's glory. If this is your commitment, then you should always show the reality of His presence in you. To that end, may His Glory always fill your temple and His Presence always be in you!

> But you…my servant…whom I have chosen, the offspring of Abraham, my friend…fear not, for I am with you; be not dismayed, for I am your God; I will strengthen you, I will help you, I will uphold you with my righteous right hand. Behold, all who are incensed against you shall be put to shame and confounded; those who strive against you shall be as nothing and shall perish…For I, the LORD your God, hold your right hand; it is I who say to you, Fear not, I am the one who helps you. (Isaiah 41:8-13,ESV – Selected)

The hymn of consecration written by Judson W. Van DeVenter (1896) expresses the relationship we are to have and maintain with the Living and Holy God.

> *All to Jesus, I surrender; All to Him I freely give;*
> *I will ever love and trust Him,*
> *In His presence daily live.*
>
> *Refrain*
>
> *I surrender all, I surrender all,*
> *All to Thee, my blessed Savior, I surrender all.*

18. Reasonable Alternative

Restore us again, O God of our salvation, and put away your indignation toward us! Will you be angry with us forever? Will you prolong your anger to all generations? Will you not revive us again, that your people may rejoice in you? Show us your steadfast love, O Lord, and grant us your salvation. Let me hear what God the Lord will speak, for he will speak peace to his people, to his saints; but let them not turn back to folly.
Psalm 85:4-8 (ESV)

  Throughout the recorded history of the Church, there are examples where the Church has experienced peaks and at other times valleys. It is difficult to predict the ebb and flow of where a Church will be at a particular moment of time. There are many factors, both internal and external, that can affect how and what a Church may experience. In a time of political unrest, the Church may experience persecution and the people of God may be exiled. In a time of the Holy Spirit's presence, there will be a time of abundant blessing and people added to the Church daily (Acts 1 through 5 contains a summary of such a time). As time passes, the Church begins to allow complacency, apathy and cultural accommodation to occur. At such a time, the Church no longer is waxing (as it should be doing) but begins a waning process (as sin and heretical concepts are embraced). What can the Church do? What should it seek after?

  The omniscient (all-knowing) God looks upon His creation and observes the institutional Church and all of its activity. What He sees and what He thinks should be of interest for all those who have affiliation with a particular Church. On the introductory page of *The Embers To A Flame* website (emberstoaflame.org), the following is stated:

Every Church needs strengthening. "And he went through Syria and Cilicia, strengthening the Churches" (Acts 15:41). God's instructions to the Church at Ephesus serve as a curriculum outline for Church vitality and revitalization: "Remember therefore from where you have fallen, and repent and do the deeds you did at first" (Revelation 2:5). There is a three-fold paradigm for renewing our Churches: Remember... Repent... Recover (Return)....

The paradigm could be paraphrased, remember to repent of all known sins so that recovery can occur and return to fellowship with the triune God will be reinstated. To begin the journey toward a reasonable alternative and transformation will require a focus on the necessity to repent. What is repentance? The website for *Desiring God* (http://www.desiringgod.org/articles/what-is-repentance) includes the following definitions:

Charles Spurgeon writes: "Repentance is a discovery of the evil of sin, a mourning that we have committed it, a resolution to forsake it. It is, in fact, a change of mind of a very deep and practical character, which makes the man love what once he hated, and hate what once he loved."

J. I. Packer writes: "Repentance means turning from as much as you know of your sin to give as much as you know of yourself to as much as you know of your God, and as our knowledge grows at these three points so our practice of repentance has to be enlarged."

There are also the instructive words of The Westminster Shorter Catechism: Question: What is repentance unto life? Answer: Repentance unto life is a saving grace, whereby a sinner, out of a true sense of his sin, and apprehension of the mercy of God in Christ, doth, with grief and hatred of his sin, turn from it unto God, with full purpose of, and endeavor after, new obedience.

Some Scriptural basis for the Catechism answer is:

Acts 11:18 (KJV), When they heard these things, they held their peace, and glorified God, saying, Then hath God also to the Gentiles granted repentance unto life.

Acts 2:37-38, Now when they heard this, they were pricked in their heart, and said unto Peter and to the rest of the apostles, Men and brethren, what shall we do? Then Peter said unto them, Repent, and be baptized every one of you in the name of Jesus Christ for the remission of sins, and ye shall receive the gift of the Holy Ghost.

Jeremiah 31:18-19, Thou hast chastised me, and I was chastised, as a bullock unaccustomed to the yoke: turn thou me, and I shall be turned; for thou art the Lord my God. Surely after that I was turned, I repented; and after that I was instructed…I was ashamed.

Psalm 119:59, I thought on my ways, and turned my feet unto thy testimonies.

Does the visible Church want to repent? Will the members of a local visible Church willingly repent of particular sins? A general guideline and motivation for dealing with sin is stated in I John. A place to begin would be the prayerful study and application of this epistle. Passages such as I John 1:8-10 (NIV), "If we claim to be without sin, we deceive ourselves and the truth is not in us. If we confess our sins, he is faithful and just and will forgive us our sins and purify us from all unrighteousness. If we claim we have not sinned, we make him out to be a liar and his word is not in us." I John 2:9 adds, "Anyone who claims to be in the light but hates a brother or sister is still in the darkness." What do these words mean and why are they significant?

We consider carefully the words in The Lord's Prayer that many congregations recite as part of their Worship ritual. The Lord's Prayer contains these words, "And forgive us our debts, as we also have forgiven our debtors" (Matthew 6:12). The operative words are forgive and forgiven. In a comparative way, if we personalize the text, it could be rendered, "Forgive me of my sins, trespasses and indebtedness to You." As we pray these words, it should cause us to look inwardly and subjectively due to our personal awareness of the many pitfalls that can cause us to sin in thought, word and deed. The text also uses the comparative with the words, "As I have forgiven others who have sinned, trespassed and been indebted to me." The point is obvious! If I sense my need of forgiveness by God, I need to exercise the spirit of forgiveness with my brothers and sisters in Christ. This is a major consideration for us because Jesus Christ added an attachment to the text we call The Lord's Prayer (Matthew 6:14-15). We should consider the words of Jesus Christ carefully and prayerfully, "For if you forgive other people when they sin against you, your heavenly Father will also forgive you. But if you do not forgive others their sins, your Father will not forgive your sins." The words are clear and precise. Jesus Christ has stated the necessity for each one of us who names His name to be a person who forgives others of their sins that have impacted us individually. If the spirit of forgiveness is not part of who we are and what we practice, it will soon fester and become compounded. One illustration is given in Ephesians 4:25-32 (NIV selected).

> Therefore each of you must put off falsehood and speak truthfully to your neighbor, for we are all members of one body. In your anger do not sin, do not let the sun go down while you are still angry, and do not give the devil

THE TWENTY-FIRST CENTURY CHURCH: IS IT WAXING OR WANING

a foothold...Do not let any unwholesome talk come out of your mouths, but only what is helpful for building others up according to their needs, that it may benefit those who listen. And do not grieve the Holy Spirit of God, with whom you were sealed for the day of redemption. Get rid of all bitterness, rage and anger, brawling and slander, along with every form of malice. Be kind and compassionate to one another, forgiving each other, just as God in Christ forgave you.

The emphasis of verse 31 is on the things we are to get rid of, "All bitterness, rage, anger, brawling, slander and every form of malice." In the Amplified Bible Online Reading Schedule (www.biblegateway.com), verse 31 is rendered, "Let all bitterness and indignation and wrath (passion, rage, bad temper) and resentment (anger, animosity) and quarreling (brawling, clamor, contention) and slander (evil-speaking, abusive or blasphemous language) be banished from you, with all malice (spite, ill will, or baseness of any kind)." The emphasis of verse 32 is on the things we are to implement and practice, "Be kind and compassionate to one another, forgiving each other, just as God in Christ forgave you." If we attach ourselves to Jesus Christ by claiming and calling ourselves "Christian", we need to take the words seriously that say, "Just as in Christ God forgave you. In The Amplified Bible Online, verse 32 is, "And become useful and helpful and kind to one another, tenderhearted (compassionate, understanding, loving-hearted), forgiving one another [readily and freely], as God in Christ forgave you." Does this describe who you are and how you live?

In most denominations and some particular Churches, there are formulations of what is vital within the visible Church. In the Presbyterian Church in America, there is a commitment to The Ordinary Means of Grace - The Word, The Sacraments (Baptism and The Lord's Supper) and Prayer. The Means of Grace is sometimes expanded to include The Biblical

Administration of Church Discipline. A proper emphasis upon and application of The Means of Grace will serve to mind us of the awfulness of sin and how repugnant it is in the sight of the Holy God. No one is fully insulated against the temptations that occur frequently in one's life. Paul stated this reality in I Corinthians 10:12-13.

> Therefore let anyone who thinks that he stands take heed lest he fall. No temptation has overtaken you that is not common to man. God is faithful, and he will not let you be tempted beyond your ability, but with the temptation he will also provide the way of escape, that you may be able to endure it.

In a previous Chapter, in the statements about Pastors and the grappling with ministry demands, the following was shared about moments when they have either been tempted or yielded to the temptation.

> Temptation itself isn't a sin, but for some reason hardly anyone talks about it openly and honestly as if talking about it were sin itself. Looking at James 1:13-16 we can clearly see the progression of temptation to sin, but for some reason people who give into temptation can't seem to find their way out and never feel safe enough to be held accountable.

In dealing with temptation, James 1:13-16 is precise and forthright.

> Let no one say when he is tempted, I am being tempted by God; for God cannot be tempted by evil, and He Himself does not tempt anyone. But each one is tempted when he is carried away and enticed by his own lust. Then when lust has conceived, it gives birth to sin; and

when sin is accomplished, it brings forth death. Do not be deceived, my beloved brethren.

On a personal basis, I have to keep reminding myself of the truths stated in Psalm 1:1-2 (NLT). There is a clearly defined pathway ordained by God for His people. If adhered to and followed, it will prevent yielding to the enticements and temptations of a secular and culturally driven society.

Oh, the joys of those who do not follow the advice of the wicked, or stand around with sinners, or join in with mockers. But they delight in the law of the Lord, meditating on it day and night.

The prerequisite for dealing with temptation is given in I John 2:12-14 (NLT). Take note of the rationale that indicates the reasons why temptations can be prevented and avoided. John wrote:

- I am writing to you who are God's children because your sins have been forgiven through Jesus.
- I am writing to you who are mature in the faith because you know Christ, who existed from the beginning.
- I am writing to you who are young in the faith because you have won your battle with the evil one.
- I have written to you who are God's children because you know the Father.
- I have written to you who are mature in the faith because you know Christ, who existed from the beginning.
- I have written to you who are young in the faith because you are strong. God's word lives in your hearts, and you have won your battle with the evil one.

The broad areas and categories of temptation are then stipulated in I John 2:15-17 (NLT). "Do not love this world nor the things it offers you, for when you love the world, you do not have the love of the Father in you." For the world offers only:

- a craving for physical pleasure,
- a craving for everything we see, and
- pride in our achievements and possessions.

These are not from the Father, but are from this world. And this world is fading away, along with everything that people crave. But anyone who does what pleases God will live forever.

It is obvious that adherence to Biblical core values will be of great benefit when confronted with the moments and situations of temptation. It will also require a purposeful commitment to the standards of God and a discipline of life that keeps one from consideration of anything questionable. A basic rule of thumb with a temptation is: "If in doubt, don't!"

For those who have yielded to temptation or succumbed to animosity toward another follower of Jesus Christ, is there a pathway to recovery, reconciliation and restoration? Jesus Christ shared with His disciples the steps to reconciliation that should be followed and taught. In Matthew 5:23-24 (ESV), "So if you are offering your gift at the altar and there remember that your brother has something against you, leave your gift there before the altar and go. First be reconciled to your brother, and then come and offer your gift." The priority and purpose of reconciliation is to settle a quarrel, dispute or difference of opinion. The challenging part of this process depends upon the one who is truly worshipping and "there you remember that your brother has something against you." At that point, you should interrupt what you are doing and seek out the person with whom there has been a quarrel or dispute. The idea is not to rehash the incident but to join together in seeking the Lord's forgiveness and the restoration of fellowship with a reconciled brother or sister in Christ.

THE TWENTY-FIRST CENTURY CHURCH: IS IT WAXING OR WANING

Jesus amplified this process further in Matthew 18:15-17 (ESV).

> If your brother sins against you, go and tell him his fault, between you and him alone. If he listens to you, you have gained your brother. But if he does not listen, take one or two others along with you, that every charge may be established by the evidence of two or three witnesses. If he refuses to listen to them, tell it to the Church. And if he refuses to listen even to the Church, let him be to you as a Gentile and a tax collector.

The last phrase, "let him be to you as a Gentile and a tax collector" is discussed in *The Pulpit Commentary* (http://biblehub.com/commentaries/matthew/18-17.htm).

> The class, not the individual, is meant. If he turns a deaf ear to the authoritative reproof of the Church, let him be regarded no longer as a brother, but as a heathen and an outcast. Christ, without endorsing the Jews' treatment of Gentiles and publicans, acknowledges the fact, and uses it as an illustration. The obdurate offender must be deprived of Church membership, and treated as those without the Jewish pale were commonly treated. The traditional law enjoined that a Hebrew might not associate, eat, or travel with a heathen, and that if any Jew took the office of publicans, he was to be virtually excommunicated.

The person who has been excluded and excommunicated can be reinstated and reconciled when repentance occurs. *The Pulpit Commentary* adds, "In later times, there naturally arose in the Christian Church the punishment of offenders by means of exclusion from holy communion, and excommunication. But even in this extreme case charity will not regard the sinner as hopelessly lost; it will seek his salvation by prayer and entreaty."

I am indebted to a man who became a friend more than fifty-five years ago. He was active with the Salvation Army and would play his musical instrument as a group did street corner evangelism. He passed along a book that I have valued all these years. It was written by James A. Stewart, an Evangelist from Scotland, and published in 1958. The title of the book is, *Come, O Breath*. In a Chapter titled, "The Sub-normal Church" he wrote:

> The vast majority of Christians are living a sub-normal Christian life. The New Testament characteristics of power invincible, joy unspeakable, glory immeasurable and peace incomprehensible are strangely lacking in their lives. The Christian experience of the Church is not deep, intense or vital enough to meet her own needs, let alone the needs of the world...We are so sickly and feeble that we are not able to discharge the functions for which we exist...We have adopted a policy of self-pity. The result is, we have the invalid's groan instead of the warrior's shout. We are absolutely powerless before the appalling conditions of the world today. The Church must herself be saved, or she cannot save the world...The Church cannot give away what she does not possess. The measure of the outward must always be a measure of the inward. It is the Church that is unbelieving, apathetic and worldly...What hurts me most is that the world does not oppose us. We are so feeble that it just ignores us.

The Lord never wanted division to occur within the visible Church. His design was that the visible Church would endeavor to be more like the invisible Church so it could effectively be light in a darkening world. A cautionary word for the visible Church is given in Galatians 5:14-15, "For the whole

THE TWENTY-FIRST CENTURY CHURCH: IS IT WAXING OR WANING

law is fulfilled in one word: You shall love your neighbor as yourself. But if you bite and devour one another, watch out that you are not consumed by one another." The choice is before us! Which one will we choose? Which choice will you make?

May the words of the Edwin Hatch Hymn (1878) be the prayer of each of us,

Breathe on me, breath of God,
Fill me with life anew,
That I may love what Thou dost love,
And do what Thou wouldst do.

Breathe on me, breath of God,
Until my heart is pure,
Until with Thee I will one will,
To do and to endure.

Breathe on me, breath of God,
Blend all my soul with Thine,
Until this earthly part of me
Glows with Thy fire divine.

About the Author

      I, the third of three children, was born in Brooklyn, New York and lived the first 20 years of my life there. In late Spring and Summer of 1954, I volunteered to be a worker at Lakeside Bible Conference in Carmel, New York. During the summer, I met several people who were already in a Bible College or preparing to enter their Freshman year. I stayed in a two-man cabin with a man who was President of the Student Body at Columbia Bible College (now Columbia International University) in Columbia, South Carolina. We had been assigned to work with teenagers from New York City. However, during the course of the summer, my roommate would frequently ask me whether or not I had ever thought about what God's will and plan for my life might be. His question "bugged" me and I did my best to avoid him and the question.

      At the end of the summer, some friends who had pre-enrolled at Columbia Bible College ,invited me to ride to South Carolina with them and then to hitch-hike back home. I had no other plans and decided to go with them. Just to "kill time" I sat in the Orientation Sessions. When I declined to receive the sheets that were distributed, a Staff Member asked me: "Why?" I indicated that I was not a student and had not enrolled. I indicated that I would be hitchhiking back to New York once the classes began. In a very gentle way, the Staff Member indicated that if I en-rolled, he and others would pray with and for me that God would provide all that was needed so I could attend the Bible College. I decided to do that and enrolled as a College Freshman. I not only received an excellent Biblical Education but in the Spring Semester (1955) one of the entering women students from Chattanooga, Tennessee arrived as a student. In the providence of God, she became my wife in 1956.

In 1958, I transferred to a new Presbyterian school, Covenant College (in St. Louis, MO, now on Lookout Mountain, GA). After graduation in 1960, I enrolled in Covenant Theological Seminary and completed my studies there in 1964. After graduation, I was called to serve as Pastor in New Jersey. I have served as a Pastor in various places in different states continuously for more than 51 years.

www.ingramcontent.com/pod-product-compliance
Lightning Source LLC
Chambersburg PA
CBHW061639040426
42446CB00010B/1488